DOVER GAME AND PUZZLE ACTIVITY BOOKS

101 Questions on How to Play Chess

FRED WILSON

D0191341

DOVER PUBLICATIONS, INC.
New York

Copyright

Copyright © 1994 by Dover Publications, Inc.
All rights reserved under Pan American and International Copyright Conventions.

Bibliographical Note

101 Questions on How to Play Chess is a new work, first published by Dover Publications, Inc., in 1994.

Edited by Alan Weissman

Library of Congress Cataloging-in-Publication Data

Wilson, Fred.
    101 questions on how to play chess / Fred Wilson.
        p.   cm.—(Dover game and puzzle activity books)
    Includes bibliographical references and index.
    ISBN 0-486-28273-2
    1. Chess—Miscellanea. I. Title. II. Title: One hundred one questions on
how to play chess. III. Series.
GV1446.W486   1994
794.1—dc20   94-34799
                                                  CIP

Manufactured in the United States of America
Dover Publications, Inc., 31 East 2nd Street, Mineola, N.Y. 11501

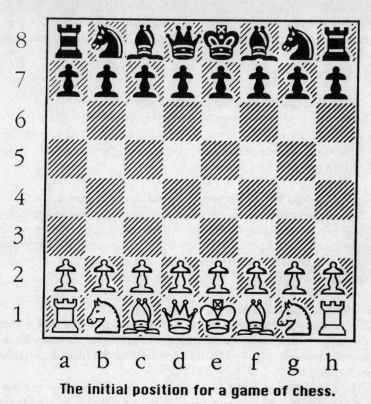

The initial position for a game of chess.

Diagram 1

1. What is the object of the game of chess?

The object of the game of chess is to checkmate your opponent's King. Checkmate occurs when either player's King is attacked and cannot escape being captured on the very next move. (In practice, the game ends without the capture actually taking place. It is enough to see that the King cannot escape.)

2. How many players take part in a game of chess?

Chess is played by two opponents. One has the White pieces, the other the Black pieces.

3. What kind of board is used?

The chessboard (which is basically the same as the one used for checkers) is made up of 64 squares, alternately colored light and dark. It contains eight vertical rows (files) of eight squares each, and eight

1

horizontal rows (ranks) of eight squares each. The squares are also often referred to as either White or Black squares (but they don't actually have to be black and white—just dark and light). All the squares can be used in play.

4. Is there a special way the board should be placed?
The players sit facing each other and the board must be placed so that a White square is in the lower right-hand corner. If this is done from the viewpoint of one player, the board as seen by the opposite player will automatically be correct as well.

5. How do you tell which player should start the game?
White always makes the first move. The players then move alternately. A player is never allowed to make two moves in a row. (There is actually a case where a player may move two pieces in quick succession, but this is considered a single move; see Question 47, below, on "castling.")

6. How do you tell which player gets White?
This is important because the player who moves first has a slight advantage. The most common method of choosing colors is for one player to conceal a White Pawn in one hand and a Black Pawn in the other hand.

His opponent taps a fist and takes the color indicated by the Pawn in that hand. If more than one game is played, the players usually take turns using the White pieces.

WHITE	BLACK	
♔	♚	1 King
♕	♛	1 Queen
♖ ♖	♜ ♜	2 Rooks
♗ ♗	♝ ♝	2 Bishops
♘ ♘	♞ ♞	2 Knights
♙ ♙ ♙ ♙ ♙ ♙ ♙	♟ ♟ ♟ ♟ ♟ ♟ ♟ ♟	8 Pawns

Diagram 2

7. How many pieces does each player have at the beginning of the game, and what are they called?
Each player has 16 pieces (there are 32 altogether), as shown in Diagram 2.

King   Queen   Bishop   Knight   Rook   Pawn

The initial or opening position of the pieces is shown in Diagram 1 (page 1). If you are unfamiliar with the way to set up the board, study this diagram carefully. This is the only correct way to set up the pieces to start a game.

Inexperienced players often transpose the initial positions of the King and Queen. A simple way to avoid this is to remember "Queen on her color." Black's Queen always starts the game on a dark square and White's Queen must begin on a light square.

Throughout this book diagrams will be used to illustrate how the pieces move, basic strategy and tactics. At the beginning of each game, White is always moving up the diagram, while Black is moving down the diagram.

8. Are there any special "tips" that can make it easier for me to learn how to play chess when using this book?
The following points are very important:

- Use a real chess set and board when studying how the pieces move and capture, and the other standard maneuvers illustrated in this book. By practicing with real chess pieces you will more quickly get a "feel" for their varied powers.
- Use a traditional chess set, made in the so-called "Staunton pattern." This is easy to identify because the pieces closely compare with the corresponding symbols used in the diagrams. This type of set is universally recognized as the easiest to play with and learn on.
- If you study these questions and answers carefully, you will find

that the basic moves of chess are not difficult to learn. Still, there are some more difficult concepts that you need to master to become a really good player. To understand these concepts, you should try to get some reinforcement from a strong amateur player (or chess teacher). On this level, it is tough to "go it" completely alone.

- Learn to use algebraic chess notation as soon as possible! Being able to "read" chess moves will greatly facilitate your progress.

9. What is chess notation?

Chess notation is a way of recording (i.e. writing down) individual chess moves in a very abbreviated and easy-to-understand manner. The two major forms of chess notation are called algebraic and descriptive. Algebraic is now by far the most popular and universally recognized, and it is the notation you will be using with this book. Descriptive was the standard notation used in English and American chess books and periodicals until about 1980. Later on, you will be introduced to descriptive notation so you may be able to enjoy the older English-language classics of chess literature.

10. What is "algebraic" chess notation?

In algebraic chess notation each square has only one name. (If you are already familiar with descriptive notation, it is important to remember this distinction.) Look at Diagram 3. Notice the vertical row of numbers on the left side, and the horizontal row of letters underneath the diagram. These are called coordinates. The numbers designate the ranks (horizontal rows of squares) while the letters designate the files (vertical rows of squares).

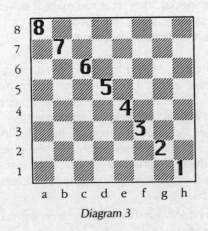

Diagram 3

11. How can I learn to use algebraic chess notation?

Look at the large, boldface numbers in the diagram. The longest White-squared diagonal on the board is illustrated with the numbers 1 through 8. This, in fact, is called the "h1–a8 diagonal." What would you call the longest diagonal row of Black squares on the board? (Answer: the "a1–h8 diagonal.") If we know that the White square with the large 4 on it is called "e4," then what are the names of the squares with a big 5 or 6 on them? (Answers: "d5" and "c6," respectively.) If the dark square immediately to the left of the big 1 is called "g1," then what are the dark squares immediately to the right of the big 7 and 8 called? (Answers: "c7" and "b8," respectively.) Simply put, you can figure out the name of any square once you determine which coordinates intersect on it.

Before moving on, choose a dozen or so squares on the diagram and practice naming them. It is important to become comfortable doing this because most chess books do not have coordinates printed on the sides of the diagrams.

12. How do I apply algebraic notation to the movements of the game?

Look at Diagram 4. Both Kings start on the "e file," with White's on the "first rank" and Black's on the "eighth rank." Therefore, we refer to the original square for White's King as "e1," and Black's as "e8."

Diagram 4

Notice that each side has already made two moves. (To remind yourself of the opening positions, refer to the diagram at the beginning of this book. In what follows, don't worry if you don't understand the moves yet. You are not expected to! Just follow along for now.) In this situation, we would say that White moved a Pawn from the square e2 to the square e4, and Black *responded* (as the traditional way of speaking describes the play) by moving a Pawn from e7 to e5. Then White moved a Knight from g1 to f3, and Black responded by bringing a Knight from b8 to c6. As you can see, this "algebraic language" makes it much easier to talk or write about how and where chess pieces move.

13. What are the abbreviations for the pieces in algebraic notation?

K	King
Q	Queen
R	Rook
B	Bishop
N	Knight

Modern algebraic notation does not use a separate abbreviation for the Pawn. The Pawn gets its name from the file it is on. Thus, at the beginning of a game, the Pawn in front of each King is known as the "*e* Pawn," (White's or Black's), and the Pawn next to it, in front of each Queen, the "*d* Pawn," and so on.

How to describe Pawn moves will be explained fully later on, but you should remember that if no symbol is given when recording a move to a given square, it must be assumed that a Pawn has been moved to that square.

14. What is meant by capturing?
In chess, you capture by removing your opponent's piece from the square it is on and replacing it with your own capturing piece.

15. How is capturing done?
All chess pieces can make captures. All chess pieces, except the King, can be captured (if a King were to be captured, that would be checkmate, and the game would be over!). If more than one capture is possible, only one of them can be made on any given move. All pieces capture the same way they would move to an empty square, except the Pawn (this notable exception will be discussed later).

16. How does the King move?
The King moves one square in any direction—forward, backward, sideways or diagonally. In Diagram 5, the King can move to any square marked with an "X."

17. How does the King capture?
The King can capture any undefended enemy piece on an *adjacent*

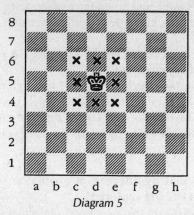

Diagram 5

square. The King can never capture a defended piece. (A piece is *defended* if the square it occupies could be immediately occupied by a piece of the same color, supposing the first piece were not there.)

In Diagram 6 White's King is on the square d4 and Black's is on e6. Black's Rook is on e3. In Diagram 7 both sides have each made one move. White has captured Black's Rook, which would be recorded as "Kxe3." The symbol "x" is universally recognized as indicating that a capture has occurred; also, in algebraic notation the piece that has been taken is not represented by name, but rather by the square it is on. Black's move, going forward one square, would be written "Ke5."

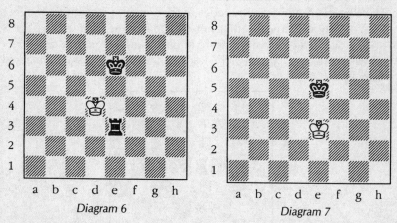

Diagram 6   Diagram 7

In Diagram 7, with White's King on e3 and Black's King on e5, if it were White's move he would have access to the squares d3, d2, e2, f2 and f3, while if it were Black's he would be able to move to d5, d6, e6, f6 and f5. No matter whose move it is, neither White nor Black could move to d4, e4 or f4, as these squares are subject to attack by an enemy piece, and you can never place your King on a square where it is under attack by any of your opponent's pieces.

18. Why is the King restricted in its ability to capture? Does this have any special significance?

It does indeed. If the King were himself to be captured, the situation would be entirely different from one in which any other single piece were captured: it would be checkmate, and the game would be over. Because of this special case, the King can never voluntarily place itself under attack.

19. Is there special significance in a situation where the King is under attack but not yet captured?

Yes. This is in fact one of the most important situations in chess. When the King is attacked and could be captured on the next move if it does not change its position or is not otherwise extricated from this situation, it is said to be in *check*. The player whose King is in check *must get his King out of check on the very next move*. (He does not necessarily have to *move* the King. If permissible, he may capture the attacking piece or, in many cases, move another piece between the attacking piece and his King.) If he cannot do this, checkmate has occurred, and the game is over!

20. How does the Rook move?

The Rook can move any number of squares in a straight line, either horizontally or vertically (but not diagonally), as long as its path is unobstructed. It can move forward or backward, but in only one direction at a time. In Diagram 8, the Rook can move to any square marked with an "X."

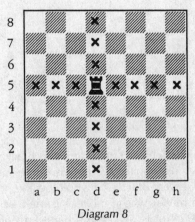

Diagram 8

21. How does the Rook capture?

It captures the same way it moves, and, as is the case with all the chess pieces, can make only one capture at a time.

22. How does the Bishop move?

The Bishop moves only on diagonals. It can move on any number of squares along a diagonal, so long as its path is not obstructed. It can move forward or backward, but in only one direction at a time. Each side has a "White-squared" Bishop and a "Black-squared" Bishop. The Bishop must remain on squares of the same color as the square it began the game on. Diagram 9 shows two Bishops of the same color. From the positions shown, each can move to any square that is of the same color as the square it now occupies and that is also marked with an "X."

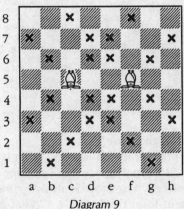

Diagram 9

23. How does the Bishop capture?

Like the Rook, the Bishop may capture any enemy piece in its path (or "line of fire"; only one capture per move, however).

24. How does the Queen move?

Like the King, the Queen can move in any direction—horizontally, vertically or diagonally (only one direction on a given move, however). The big difference between them, however, is while the King can only move one square at a time, the Queen can move as many squares as you want it to along a straight line, as long as its path is not obstructed. As is sometimes emphasized, the Queen combines the powers of the Rook and the Bishop.

25. How does the Queen capture?

The Queen captures the same way it moves and can capture any enemy piece within its line of fire. The Queen is by far the most powerful piece on the chessboard and, after the King, the most important. If you place a Queen on any of the four central squares of an empty board (e4, d4, e5 or d5) you can see that it controls no fewer than 28 of the 64 squares! (Where the "X"s are marked in Diagram 10.) Unless you have sacrificed it to force mate ("mate" is an abbreviation for "checkmate"), losing your Queen for small compensation almost always means you have stumbled into a lost position.

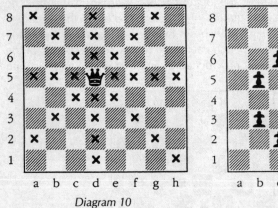

Diagram 10

Diagram 11

26. How does the Knight move?

The Knight's move is a bit difficult to learn, but it is also the most fun!

This is because it is the only piece that can jump over other pieces. Also, it is the only piece whose move is always of the same length, that is, three squares that form the letter "L." What often confuses the beginner is that the "L" can be sideways, backward or upside down! Technically, the Knight's move may be described as (a) one square forward or backward and then two squares to either side; or (b) one square to either side and then two squares forward or backward. The Knight is really moving from one corner of a 3 × 2 rectangle to the corner farthest away, and should always land on a square of a different color than the one it started on.

27. How does the Knight capture?

The Knight captures the same way it moves and, as is true of all chess pieces, can never land on a square already occupied by one of its own men.

In Diagram 11 the Knight on d4 is able to capture any of the eight Black Pawns. This is an example of how many squares a centrally posted Knight can control. Interestingly, both a Knight or a King placed on d4 will each control the same number of squares, eight, though they are completely different ones. Because of the Knight's greater range, it is considered to be slightly more powerful as an aggressive piece than a King. In general, two Bishops are a bit stronger than two Knights, as in a wide open position they can control more territory. However, in blocked positions, Knights, which can leap over both their own and enemy pieces, are generally a little superior. Note that, owing to the special way a Knight moves and captures, when your King is checked by a Knight you *cannot* get him out of check by moving a piece *between* the attacking Knight and your King!

28. How does the Pawn move?

The Pawn is a unique piece for several reasons. A Pawn can move only forward, never backward. Nor can a Pawn ever move sideways (horizontally). The Pawn moves straight ahead, only one square at a time, with one important exception: you may move a Pawn *one or two squares* on its *first* move. After its first move a Pawn can only move one square at a time! In any case, however, although you have the option of moving a Pawn one or two squares forward from its starting position, you may do so only if the squares are empty (i.e., not occupied by one of your pieces or your opponent's). In Diagram 12, the White Pawn (on square e2, *its starting square*) can move to either of the squares in front of it marked with an "X." The Black Pawn (on square c6), no longer on its starting square, can move *only* to the one square in front of it marked with an "X."

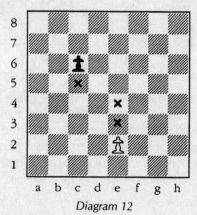

Diagram 12

29. Why can't the Pawn move to an occupied square in front of it by capturing the piece in its way?

The Pawn is the only piece that captures differently from the way it moves! That's right, even though Pawns can only move straight ahead if there is an empty square in front of them, they cannot capture anything that may be on the square directly in front of them. A Pawn can only capture diagonally, one square ahead. For example, if White has a Pawn on the square c4, it can only capture enemy pieces that may be on b5 or d5.

30. Is there anything else about the Pawn that makes it unique?

Yes! When a Pawn advances completely across the board and reaches the last rank it may legally move to, it becomes another piece! This is called Pawn *promotion*. A promoted Pawn must become another piece, and can never remain a Pawn or become a King.[1] A Pawn may be promoted to a Queen, Rook, Bishop or Knight, although, in actual practice, 99 percent of the time you should promote to a Queen, as the Queen is by far the most powerful piece. And, yes, this does mean that you can have two, or even three or four Queens at the same time! For one side to have more than two simultaneously, however, is rare.

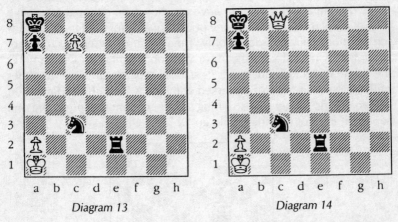

Diagram 13   *Diagram 14*

In Diagram 13, Black threatens mate in one move by 1. ... Rxa2++, but it is White's move. White promotes his *c* Pawn (written as 1. c8=Q++), mating Black first (Diagram 14)! (In the above notation, notice that the moves are numbered to make it easy to remember at what point in the game a move was made. When Black's move is given by itself it is always preceded by three ellipsis dots. "++" stands for "checkmate.")

1. You should be aware that, unless explained otherwise, "pieces" in chess writing always means Knights, Bishops, Rooks and Queens—*not* Pawns. Up to now, for instructional purposes, I have been loosely referring to Pawns as "pieces." In the literature, however, Pawns are always referred to as Pawns. The *minor pieces* are Bishops and Knights. The *major pieces* are Queens and Rooks.

31. In algebraic notation, if both of the same pieces of the same type and color can move to the same square, how can you tell which one moved there?

When two of the same type of piece can move to the same square, you should try to indicate which one you are moving by giving the letter for the file it is on after the abbreviation for the piece itself. For example, in Diagram 15, if White wanted to attack Black's Pawn on c6 with his Knight on f3, you would write 1. Nfe5, and if Black wanted to defend the c6 Pawn with his Rook on f8, he would move 1. ... Rfc8. If Black had defended the c6 Pawn with the other Rook you would write 1. ... Rbc8.

Diagram 15

However, if both pieces are on the same file, then you write the rank the piece is on after the abbreviation for the piece being moved. In the position shown in Diagram 15, after the moves 1. Nfe5 Rfc8, if White wanted to attack the c6 Pawn again with his Rook on the first rank, he would write 2. R1a6. If he had used the other Rook, it would be written 2. R7a6.

32. If I can make a capture with either of two Pawns, which one is usually correct?

Nine out of ten times you should make Pawn captures towards the center.

33. Now how about some examples showing how to use the major pieces? For instance, how do I use the Bishop to capture and check?

(Before we proceed, let me make a very strong suggestion. You should play out these examples—and all those that follow—on a chessboard with real chess pieces. It's the only way to learn!) Diagrams 16 to 19 illustrate how the Bishops move, capture and check. In Diagram 16, it

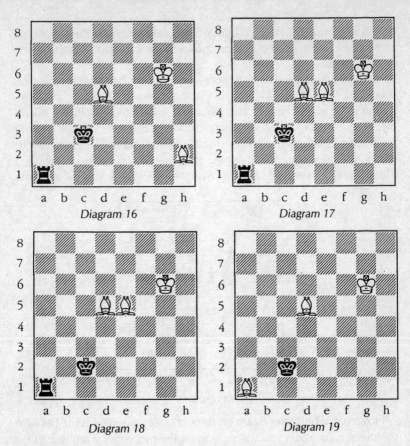

Diagram 16

Diagram 17

Diagram 18

Diagram 19

is White's move. In Diagram 17 White has moved 1. Be5+. (The symbol "+" means "check" in algebraic notation.) In Diagram 18, Black, being forced to move his King out of check, has replied 1. ... Kc2. In Diagram 19 White's Bishop captures Black's undefended Rook by 2. Bxa1. This tactical maneuver, attacking the King diagonally and winning an undefended piece behind it, is known as a *skewer*.

The position in Diagram 19 is hopelessly lost for Black, as White can eventually force mate with a King and two Bishops against a lone King. By using his King in combination with the two Bishops, White can slowly but surely force Black's King to the side of the board and mate him in a corner. However, a King and only one Bishop cannot force checkmate. Such a game would be a draw.

34. Can you give me some examples of how the Rook is used?

In Diagram 20 the Rook on e4 has the option of going to any of the squares on either the fourth rank or the *e* file. In Diagram 21 White's

Rook on d3 is attacking (checking) not only Black's King on a3, but also the Pawn on h3. After Black's King's forced move out of the line of fire (to either a2 or b2), White's Rook can take Black's Pawn (Rxh3).

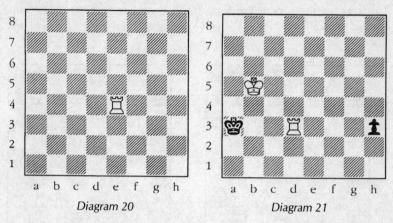

Diagram 20

Diagram 21

Rooks work especially well together when they defend each other, and their attacking power is significantly increased. In Diagram 22 it is White's move, and with his doubled Rooks on the *e* file he can win almost immediately.

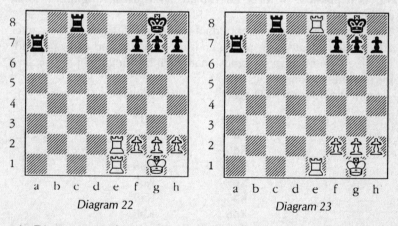

Diagram 22

Diagram 23

In Diagram 23 White has moved his Rook from e2 to e8 (written as "1. Re8+"), checking Black's King. In Diagram 24 Black's forced reply is 1. ... Rxe8, as there is no other way for him to get his King out of check.

Now, what does White do (see Diagram 25)?

Answer: White's move, 2. Rxe8++, is checkmate! Why? Because Black's King is in check and he cannot get out of check on the very next move. Black cannot capture the attacking piece. Black cannot interpose one of his pieces to block the White Rook's attack on his King. Black cannot move his King out of the White Rook's line of fire. This type of mate with the King trapped on the first or eighth rank behind several of his Pawns is very common and is called a *back-rank mate*.

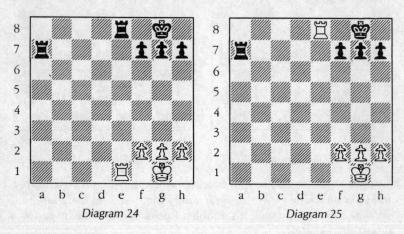

Diagram 24   Diagram 25

35. Is it possible to force checkmate with just a King and a Rook against a King?

Yes. In fact, this is a very important maneuver to learn. Many games are decided because one player ends up a Rook ahead and, after trading off all the other pieces, must mate with his King and Rook against his opponent's lone King.

From the position in Diagram 26, White to play . . .

1.	**Re6+**	**Kd7**
2.	**Kd5**	**Kc7**
3.	**Rd6**	**Kb7**
4.	**Rc6**	**Kb8**
5.	**Kc5**	**Kb7**
6.	**Kb5**	**Ka8**
7.	**Kb6**	**Kb8**
8.	**Rc5 (or any other safe square on the *c* file)**	
8.	**. . .**	**Ka8**
9.	**Rc8++** (see Diagram 27)	

This is a standard King + Rook mate. By using your King and Rook in conjunction, with the King often defending the Rook, you can always drive your opponent's King to the edge of the board, by taking squares away from him, and force mate in a corner.

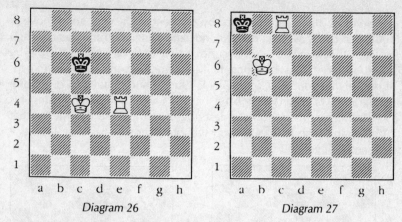

Diagram 26   Diagram 27

It is a good idea to practice mating with a King and Rook against a friend until you feel comfortable doing it. This type of *endgame* (later we will learn more about the endgame and other special parts of a game of chess) is very common and, while an experienced player will usually resign in such an obviously lost position, beginners will always make you play it out.

(Experienced players rarely play a game to the end if it is clear that it is impossible for one of them to win. The losing player will then *resign*, that is, concede the game to his or her opponent.)

36. Can you illustrate some ways in which the Queen moves and captures?

Certainly. In Diagram 28 it is White's move. White is a piece down (a Bishop) and would be glad to draw. Therefore White moves his Queen diagonally to d4, attacking Black's King and Bishop (Qd4+!). (See Diagram 29.)

Diagram 28

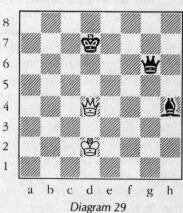

Diagram 29

(Note: In algebraic notation, by convention, a very good move is indicated by "!" while a mistake, not surprisingly, is followed by a "?")

Then Black makes the only move that both defends his King, by interposition (that is, blocking the King), and prevents White from capturing his Bishop: Black moves his Queen horizontally to d6 (Qd6). (Diagram 30.) Now White sees that his Queen is *pinned* against his own King (as this position is described): in this case this means that White can't take Black's Bishop without exposing his King to check (which is illegal).

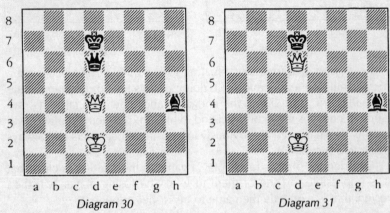

Diagram 30   Diagram 31

Therefore he plays Qxd6+ and it is a draw (Diagram 31). Why is the position after Qxd6+ a draw? Because after Black's only reasonable reply, ... Kxd6, neither side has sufficient material to force mate. (Try to figure out why this is so. Hint: a Bishop can never attack a piece on a square of a different color.)

37. How do you force checkmate with Queen and King against a King?

This is also a very common and important endgame situation and, although it is a bit simpler to do than mating with King and Rook, the overall strategy of driving the enemy King to the edge of the board where it will be cornered and mated, is the same. However, since the Queen is so powerful, you can use it alone to restrain your opponent's King, and gradually take away most of the squares it could flee to. A sample variation is given in Diagrams 32 and 33.

In Diagram 32, with White on the move, play might continue:

1. Qe4 Kc5 2. Qd3 Kc6 3. Qd4 Kc7 4. Qd5 Kb6 5. Qc4 Kb7 6. Qc5 Ka8!

(In this lost position, Black sets one last trap for White. If White were now to play either 7. Qb6? or 7. Qc7?, the game would be a draw because, although it is Black's move, his King is not under attack and he has no legal moves. This is called a *stalemate*.) 7. Qe7! (restricting Black's King to the edge of the board, in this case, the eighth rank; the rest is easy with White bringing up his King to aid his Queen in delivering checkmate) 7. ... Kb8 8. Kc3 Kc8 9. Kb4 Kb8 10. Kb5 Ka8 11. Kb6 Kb8. (Diagram 33.) Now White can give mate with his Queen on four different squares. Can you find them? (Answer: d8, e8, f8 and b7, where the Queen is defended by White's King.)

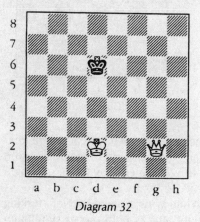

Diagram 32

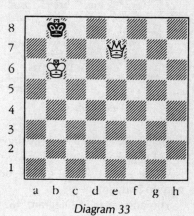

Diagram 33

38. What is a Knight fork?

Diagram 34 above shows an example of what is called a Knight fork. Black has just moved to d3 (Nd3 +), checking White's King and attacking his Queen *at the same time*. After White's forced move of K f1, if you were Black, what would you do—take White's Queen, thus creating an even position with "material equality," or something else? ANSWER: This is a bit of a trick question because normally playing

Diagram 34

19

...Nxb2 would be best. But look a little harder because after Kf1 Black has...Re1++ (checkmate!).

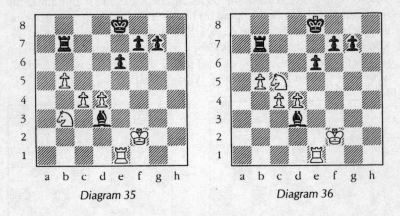

Diagram 35   Diagram 36

Diagrams 35 and 36 show another example of a typical Knight fork:

In Diagram 35 both sides have an equal amount of material, and it is White's move. What can he do to win material by force, gaining a winning advantage?

The answer is in Diagram 36. White wins a piece by Nc5, forking Black's Rook and Bishop. The Knight attacks both pieces simultaneously, and neither piece can defend the other.

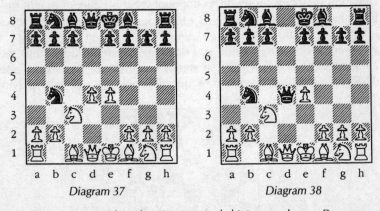

Diagram 37   Diagram 38

In Diagram 37 White has just moved d4 (remember, a Pawn move is designated by only recording the square it is moving to). Is this move a tactical error or not? Answer: Yes! It is a big mistake, as Black can play ... Qxd4! (Diagram 38) winning a Pawn at no cost. Worse yet, if White goes Qxd4, Black has ... Nc2+, forking White's King *and* Queen!

39. Can I use this forking effect with any other piece?

Yes. It can even be used with a Pawn, which, as noted, is not considered a "piece." Examine Diagram 39:

In this position it is White's move. Although a piece down (Black has a Knight), he remembers his options with the Pawn's first move. What can he play? White plays 1. c4!, attacking both Black's Rook and Knight. (Diagram 40.) This is called a Pawn fork. Black must lose one of his pieces for a Pawn.

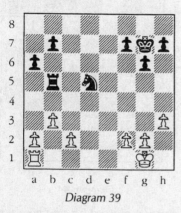

Diagram 39

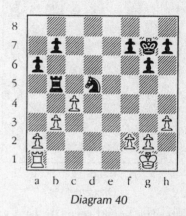

Diagram 40

Black sensibly plays 1. ... Rc5, saving his Rook (Diagram 41). A Rook is slightly stronger than a Knight, as it usually controls more squares, and it is therefore more valuable. White responds by playing "Pawn takes Knight," which is written as 2. cxd5 (note that here the conventions of algebraic notation require that the Pawn be identified somehow, to avoid confusion; it is identified by the letter of the *file* it occupies). This trade is a good deal for White, as a Knight is generally worth about three Pawns. (Diagram 42.)

Diagram 41

Diagram 42

In Diagram 43 it is Black's move.

a. How many different Pawn captures can Black make?

b. Is Black's strongest move to take White's Queen on e4 (dxe4)?

Answers: a. Black has five possible Pawn captures (cxb5, dxc4, dxe4, exf4 and fxg5).

b. Normally winning a Queen for only a Pawn is terrific, but cxb5++ is checkmate! (Diagram 44.)

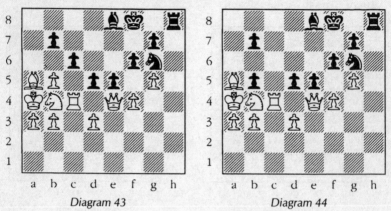

Diagram 43   Diagram 44

40. The Knight seems to be a very unusual piece. Can you give me any more ideas about how to use the Knight?

Here are some more tips about how best to use the Knight:

- At the beginning of a game it is usually a good idea to develop Knights from their initial squares towards the center (to *develop* a piece means to move it into a more advantageous position). This is because Knights control much more territory from central squares such as f3 and c3, or f6 and c6, than from "edge squares" like a3, h3, a6 or h6.

- Even though a Knight and a Bishop are considered to be "more or less" equal in value, except in very blocked positions, two Bishops almost always control more squares than two Knights or a Bishop and Knight, and their possession constitutes a slight advantage. Therefore it is often wise to try and trade one of your Knights for one of your opponent's Bishops, or encourage him to do so.

- Not only can you not force checkmate with a King and one Knight, but you cannot force mate with a King and two Knights! Although your opponent may blunder into a mate, try to avoid being left with only a King and two Knights near the end of a game.

41. Is there a "special" kind of checkmate that only a Knight can do?

Yes! It is called a *smothered mate*, and one version of it known as *Philidor's Legacy*[2] was recently pulled off by the World Champion Gary Kasparov against Grandmaster Matthias Wahls in 1992, as shown in Diagrams 45–54 (Kasparov played White, Wahls Black).

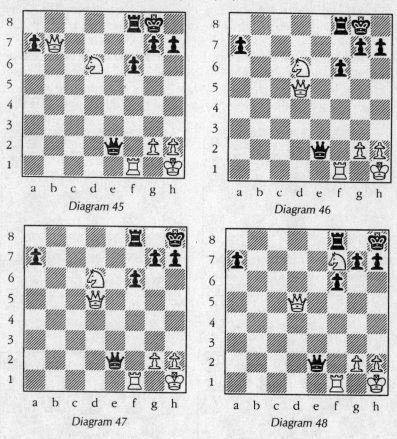

Diagram 45

Diagram 46

Diagram 47

Diagram 48

From the position in Diagram 45 White initiates a winning tactical maneuver by 1. Qd5+ (1. Qb3+ would lead to the same thing).

Diagram 46: after 1. Qd5+ Black cannot interpose by 1. ... Rf7 because 2. Qxf7+ Kh8 3. Qf8++ is mate.

Therefore Black must play 1. ... Kh8 (Diagram 47), but White has a clever rejoinder.

White's move is 2. Nf7+ (Diagram 48), forcing Black to play 2. ...

2. François Philidor (1726–1795), whose name appears again and again in chess writings, was the greatest chess player of the eighteenth century.

Kg8 (Diagram 49). Why? Because if Black captured White's Knight, White would have mate in three moves beginning with 3. Qd8+.

Now White has available a very powerful attacking move. Do you see it?

Look at Diagram 50: 3. Nh6+ is a *double check*, as both White's Queen and Knight are attacking Black's King simultaneously. When you are being double checked, you must move your King. (Black's reply cannot be 3. ... Rf7, as his King would still be in check!)

After Black's forced move of 3. ... Kh8 (Diagram 51) White has an extraordinary move available. Do you see a sacrifice that forces mate?

Now look at Diagram 52: White makes the amazing move 4. Qg8+!, to which Black has only one legal reply. Black must play 4. ...

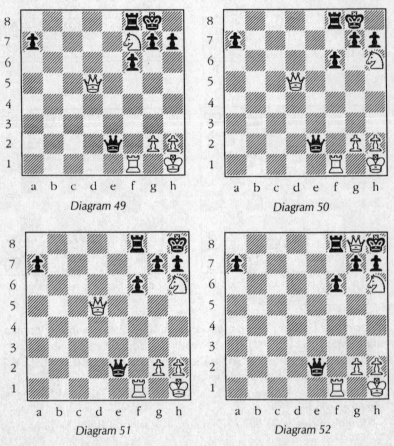

Diagram 49

Diagram 50

Diagram 51

Diagram 52

Rxg8 (Diagram 53) because 4. ... Kxg8 is illegal as Black's King would then be in check from White's Knight on h6. Notice that now Black's

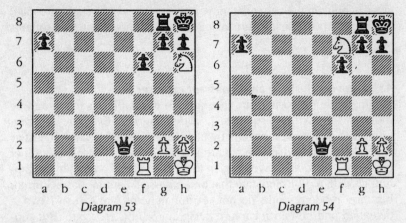

Diagram 53   Diagram 54

King is completely surrounded and trapped by his own men, and he has no flight square. Also, Black's Rook no longer controls f7.

Diagram 54: White now plays 5. Nf7++ checkmate! Not only is Black's King attacked and left without a legal move, but also none of his pieces can capture White's Knight. This type of maneuver, where you sacrifice material either to improve your position or to establish a won game, is called a *combination*.

42. Is there another unusual way I can use a Pawn to make a capture?

Yes. A Pawn can also capture in a special way called capturing *en passant* (French for "in passing"). This is a bit tricky but very important to learn. The following conditions are required for a Pawn to capture *en passant*:

a. *En passant* captures only involve Pawns. An *en passant* capture is always that of a Pawn capturing another Pawn.

b. A Pawn may capture *en passant* only when it has already moved three squares forward from its original square. In other words, a White Pawn may capture *en passant* only when it is on the fifth rank, and a Black Pawn only when it is on the fourth rank.

c. As in "normal" Pawn captures, you can only capture *en passant* if the Pawn to be captured is on an adjacent file and your capturing Pawn will end up one square diagonally forward as usual.

d. The only Pawn you may capture *en passant* is one that has just taken the option of moving two squares on its first move. For example, if White has a Pawn on e5 and Black attempts to move a Pawn from f7 to f5 in one move, White has the option of taking Black's *f* Pawn *as if it had moved only to f6* (and White's Pawn ends the capture on f6). This option must be used *immediately*. That is, you can capture *en*

25

passant only on the very next move after your opponent has attempted to evade a possible capture of his Pawn by moving it two squares instead of one.

43. Can you illustrate an *en passant* capture?

Starting with the position in Diagram 55, if it is Black's move and he moves his *f* Pawn two squares (1. ... f5; Diagram 56) White can capture Black's *f* Pawn *en passant* by playing 2. exf6 (Diagram 57), just as if Black had moved it one square instead of two. (Note: many older books and periodicals would give the initials "e.p." after White's capture [2. exf6 e.p.] to indicate that an *en passant* capture has occurred, but most modern works do not.) Fortunately for Black, his *f* Pawn is defended and he can *recapture* (Diagram 58) by 2. ... gxf6. But sup-

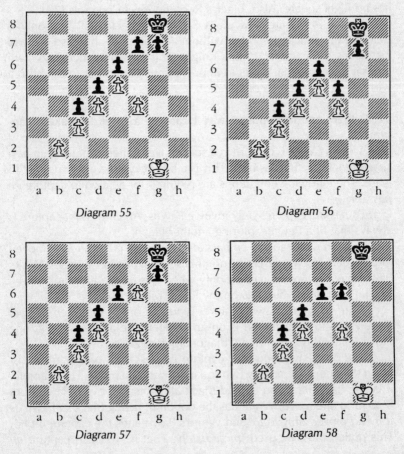

Diagram 55

Diagram 56

Diagram 57

Diagram 58

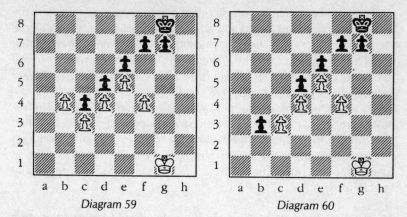

Diagram 59   Diagram 60

pose it is White's move in Diagram 55, and he plays 1. b4 (see Diagram 59).

What do you think is Black's best reply? Black's best move is 1. ... cxb3 (Diagram 60), capturing *en passant*, winning White's unprotected *b* Pawn without giving up a thing!

It is important to emphasize that the *en passant* capture is optional, not compulsory. You should choose to make an *en passant* capture not just because you can, but only if you believe it will improve your position.

44. Why was the *en passant* capture created?

Chess is a very old game, probably originating in India during the sixth century A.D. During the early days of chess, Pawns could move only one square at a time under any circumstances. Later, as chess became popular in Europe, several changes in the rules of the original game (which had been originally named *Chaturanga*) were introduced to "speed up" the game. Among these changes were the option of a Pawn's moving two squares on its first move and that of "castling" (we will discuss castling in Question 47). The *en passant* rule was created during the fifteenth century because before that time a Pawn on its original square could not move two squares at once to avoid possibly being captured by a hostile Pawn on an adjacent file. The *en passant* rule thus retained an aspect of the earlier game; now a Pawn on its original square *still* cannot avoid capture in this way!

45. Is there anything else I should know about Pawn promotion?

Pawn promotion is a very important concept. Despite being the weakest chess pieces (remember, though, that in describing play, Pawns are never referred to as "pieces") Pawns are still quite important because any one of them might become a new Queen. Over fifty percent of the time if you lose a Pawn with no compensation you will eventually lose the game. If your opponent has an extra Pawn, and he is able to bring about even trades of all the remaining pieces and Pawns, you will have only a King left, but he will have a King and a potential Queen! Incidentally, a common way of describing how you have promoted a Pawn to a Queen is to say you have "Queened" a Pawn. The renowned chess author Fred Reinfeld once wrote that if "checkmating your opponent is the strongest move in chess . . . [then] queening a Pawn successfully is the second strongest move . . . , for this signifies an enormous gain in material . . . and . . . makes victory practically certain for you."

46. If Queening a Pawn is so terrific, why should I ever promote a Pawn to anything else?

There are a variety of tactical reasons for this. For the most common, examine Diagram 61.

It is White's move. He is behind in material, as he has only one Pawn for a Knight (what this means is that, although White has one Pawn more than Black, Black has one Knight remaining while White has lost both Knights). However, it is a *passed* Pawn (that is, one that can no longer be captured and prevented from Queening by an enemy Pawn). But it is being attacked by Black's Queen, which is threatening to take it (1. ... Qxc7), and White is unable to defend it (e.g., if White plays 1. Qc4 to defend his passed Pawn on c7, Black plays 1. ... Nxc4, winning White's Queen). There is no point in White's trying to Queen his c7 Pawn now, as Black would simply take it with his Knight (1. c8=Q Nxc8). So what is White to do? The answer is that White plays 1. Qxd6! (see Diagram 62). After Black's only reasonable response,

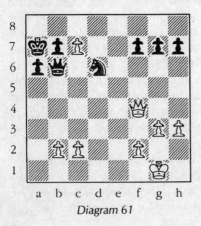

Diagram 61

Diagram 62

28

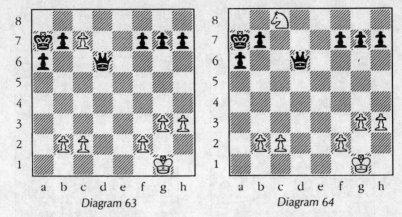

Diagram 63   Diagram 64

1. ... Qxd6 (Diagram 63), what would you do—play 2. c8=Q, thus establishing material equality, or something else? Now look at Diagram 64. White, instead of Queening his Pawn, promotes it to a *Knight* by playing 2. c8=N+!, *forking* Black's King and Queen. After 2. ... Kb8 3. Nxd6, White wins some Black Pawns and will thus still have a chance to promote a Pawn to a new Queen, and before Black can do the same!

Another reason not to promote a Pawn to a Queen is to avoid a possible stalemate. Usually then promoting to a Rook is good enough. (Promoting to a Bishop is almost never the best move available.)

47. What is "castling"?

Castling involves a move with the King and one of the Rooks. This is the only "double move" allowed in a game of chess, the only time you are allowed to move two pieces at the same time. Nevertheless, these two moves together are considered to constitute *only a single move.* You can castle only if your King and Rook are on their original squares, and neither piece has moved previously.

48. How is castling done?

Castling is a two-part operation. First, you move your King two squares horizontally along the rank toward a Rook. Then you move that Rook to the other side of the King and place it on the square immediately next to the King. If White castles to his *right* he castles *Kingside,* and if he goes to his *left* he castles *Queenside.* With Black this is reversed: he castles *Kingside* on his *left* and *Queenside* on his *right.* When you castle, the King always moves only two squares, and the Rook two squares when castling Kingside (e.g., from h1 to f1) and three squares when castling Queenside (e.g., from a1 to d1). In both algebraic and descriptive notation Kingside castling is written as "0-0" and Queenside castling is written as "0-0-0." Study Diagrams 65 through 68.

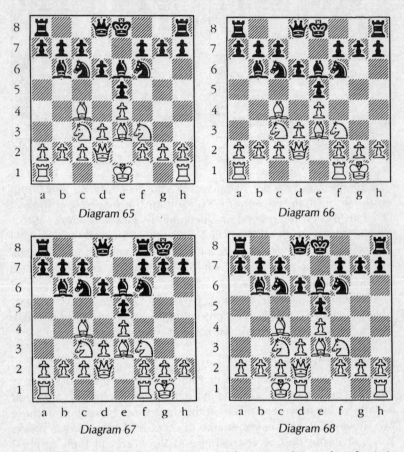

Diagram 65

Diagram 66

Diagram 67

Diagram 68

In Diagram 65, after seven reasonable moves for each side, it is White's move. White chooses to castle Kingside. This would be written as "8. 0-0" (Diagram 66).

Black follows suit and also decides to castle Kingside: 8. ... 0-0 (Diagram 67). If, on his eighth move, White had chosen to castle Queenside, the position would be as in Diagram 68 (written as "8. 0-0-0").

49. Under what conditions is it forbidden to castle?

- You cannot castle if you have already moved your King (even if it has since returned to its original square).

30

- You cannot castle if you have already moved the Rook you are castling with (even if it has since returned to its original square).
- You cannot castle to get out of check. If your King is in check you must first deal with the situation in the usual way, either by capturing the attacking enemy piece or through interposition, before castling on a subsequent move.
- You cannot castle into check! As with ordinary King moves, you can never castle your King onto a square attacked by one of your opponent's men, because this would be placing your own King in check.
- You cannot castle through check, that is, you cannot castle if your King has to pass over a square controlled by an enemy piece. Interestingly, you *are* allowed to castle if your castling Rook is being attacked, as long as your King does not move through or land on a square attacked by one of your opponent's men.
- You cannot castle if any of the squares between your King and castling Rook are occupied, either by your own or enemy pieces. However, if the squares in question become vacant, you are free to castle if all the other requirements are fulfilled.

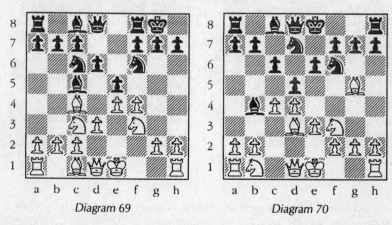

Diagram 69   *Diagram 70*

Examine the positions in Diagrams 69 and 70 above and try to determine whether or not in each situation castling would be legal:

In Diagram 69, it is White's move. Can he castle? Answer: No, as the Queenside is blocked by his own men, and castling Kingside would place his King in check!

In Diagram 70, it is White's move. Can he castle? Answer: No, because he is in check from Black's Bishop on b4. He must first reply to this check.

50. How do I decide whether to castle or not?

Let's think about it. Can, and should, White castle in the positions shown in Diagrams 71 through 74?

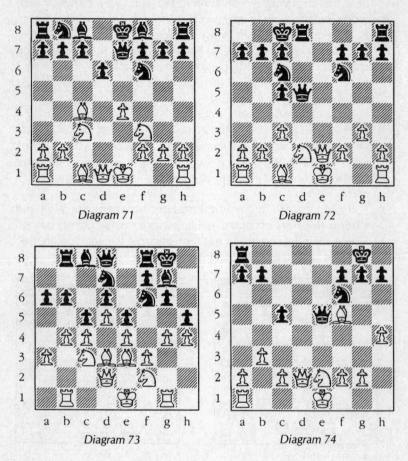

Diagram 71   Diagram 72

Diagram 73   Diagram 74

Diagram 71: Yes, Kingside castling is legal and is, in fact, White's best move. At first glance it would appear that White loses a Pawn if he castles because if 1. 0-0 Nxe4 2. Nxe4 Qxe4, and Black has won a Pawn. However, if you look one move farther you may see that White has 3. Re1, pinning Black's Queen to his King. Black's Queen cannot move off the *e* file because it would expose his King to check. His only reasonable reply is 3. ... Qxe1+, but as a result he must lose his Queen for a Rook (4.Qxe1+), giving White a winning advantage. The pin is a very common tactic and you must always be on the look-out for it.

Diagram 72: Yes, Kingside castling is not only legal but essential! Any other move by White loses significant material immediately. Black threatens White in two separate ways: he could (1) capture White's undefended Rook on h1 with his Queen on d5, or (2) pin White's Queen to his King on the open *e* file by moving either of his Rooks to e8. White's only move that would defend against both threats is 1. 0-0. Then, even though Black has the better *development* (i.e., Black has more pieces moved from their original squares to more aggressive posts), White can fight on.

The positions illustrated in Diagram 72 are called *open* positions. Generally, in open positions the central files, particularly the *d* and *e* files, are either completely open or at least "semiopen." Open positions are also distinguished by the fact that they provide the so-called "long range" pieces (Queen, Rook and Bishop) with more scope. (For more on open and semiopen positions see the note to Question 57, below.) The next diagram (73) has an example of a closed position.

Diagram 73: No, White cannot castle, as he has already moved both of his Rooks. Notice that this is a *closed* position, that is, a position where the central files are blocked by interlocking Pawns. Also, in this position, White is attacking on both the Queenside and the Kingside. In a situation like this his King is actually *safer* in the center. Therefore, White's best move is probably 1. Ke2, "connecting" his Rooks.

Diagram 74: Yes, White can castle Queenside if he so chooses, but it would be a terrible mistake because if 1. 0-0-0?? then 1. ... Qa1++—checkmate! So what should White do in this tricky position? Although he has an extra piece (the Bishop on f5) it would seem that White will have to give it back, since Black's Queen on e5 is attacking both White's Bishop and Rook simultaneously (as well as his defended Knight). However, if White plays 1. Rd1!, Black cannot capture the Bishop safely. Why? (Answer: If Black moves 1. ... Qxf5??, then White has 2. Qd8+! Rxd8 3. Rxd8+ Ne8 4. Rxe8++ mate! This is another example of a back-rank mate.)

51. Why should you want to castle, anyway?

As you have seen, the paramount objective in a game of chess is to checkmate your opponent's King. Now, the center of the board and the central files make up the area where the pieces have their greatest mobility. Consequently, the King is more apt to find himself in a crossfire between the enemy's pieces and his own if he remains on his original square. Therefore, castling is an important means of protecting your King and should usually be played as early as possible, especially in open positions.

Also, if your King remains on his original square he is much more likely to obstruct the movement of your pieces. If he is castled, he will be out of the way, safely "tucked in a corner," so to speak, giving your pieces more effective maneuvering room.

Another interesting fact about castling is that Queenside castling occurs far less often than Kingside castling. Possibly this is because after either side has castled, the *a* Pawn is often totally undefended. At any rate, statistically speaking, White only castles Queenside about one-third of the time, while Black even less so, perhaps only one-fifth of the time.

52. Can castling also be an aggressive, attacking move?

Yes. It is easy to imagine either side castling Queenside and simultaneously checking the enemy King, when it is on the open *d* file, with the castling Rook. There is also a related combination in which both your King and castling Rook attack two of your opponent's pieces simultaneously. This is illustrated in the position in Diagram 75, from a correspondence game[3] between Robert McCrary and Selig Wassner in 1983.

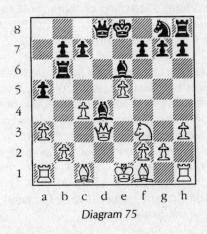

Diagram 75

It was Black's move. He had sacrificed a Pawn earlier and now hoped to recover equality of material by initiating the following combination, beginning with 13. ... Bxb2. (Diagram 76.) Was this correct?

It would appear to have been, since, after 14. Qxd8+ Kxd8 15. Bxb2 Rxb2, hadn't Black equalized the game, having won his Pawn back? (Diagram 77.)

3. *Correspondence chess* is chess played by mail. Correspondence games usually take anywhere from six months to two years to complete.

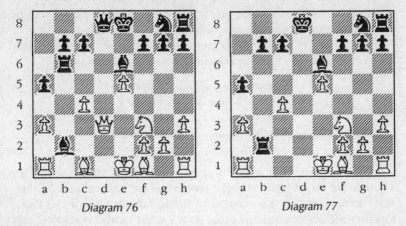

| Diagram 76 | Diagram 77 |

No! Because White played 16. 0-0-0+!, simultaneously checking Black's King with his Rook, while attacking Black's Rook with his King. (Diagram 78.) Black now *resigned*. That is, he conceded the game to White because he stood to lose a Rook for nothing, and (these were very experienced players) knew that from that point on he could not win against White's stronger position. Remember, a player's first obligation is to move his King out of check, and therefore Black could not protect his Rook.

Diagram 78

53. What are the relative values of the pieces on the chessboard?
This is a question that can be asked constantly during a game of chess. It arises every time there is a possibility of gaining or losing by an exchange of pieces or Pawns. If you gain by such exchanges, you may end up with enough extra *material* (pieces and Pawns with a greater total value than your opponent's) to be sure of winning the game. If

you lose by such exchanges, you are likely to lose the game through inability to parry your opponent's threats.

The following table assigns approximate values to all the pieces (with the exception of the King, of course, whose value is infinite):

Queen ....9 points
Rook ....5 points
Bishop ....3 points
Knight..........................3 points
Pawn ....1 point

From this table you can see that you can readily trade a Bishop for a Knight (or vice versa), as these pieces are basically of equal value. You can also see that, for example, a Rook, a minor piece and a Pawn together are about equal in value to a Queen, and, in practice, this tends to be true. Two Rooks are often, but not always, thought to be slightly more valuable than a Queen. This is particularly true in situations where the side with two Rooks has a safely placed King, and there are enemy Pawns that the Rooks can attack twice (that is, both Rooks can attack simultaneously) but the Queen can defend only once.

54. Do the values in this table always hold good?
In the vast majority of cases you will find this table of relative values a reliable guide to all types of captures and exchanges. There are times, however, when it is advantageous to give up material—part with a more valuable piece in return for a less valuable piece (or even a Pawn) or even no piece at all. Such a move is called a *sacrifice*. The idea behind a sacrifice is being able to achieve some goal that is more important than the loss of material involved.

Thus while it is catastrophic to lose a Queen or a Rook without material compensation, if you can force checkmate by sacrificing one (or both) of these powerful pieces, obviously then you can ignore the table!

55. What is meant by losing or sacrificing "the exchange"?
As you can see from the table under Question 53, a Rook is worth more than a Bishop or a Knight. When you win a Rook in return for a Bishop or a Knight (for example), you are said to "win the exchange." If you lose a Rook for a Bishop or a Knight, you are said to "lose the exchange." If you purposely give up a Rook for a Bishop or a Knight in the hope of obtaining good compensation, you are said to "sacrifice the exchange."

Two good reasons for sacrificing the exchange are either to obtain a winning mating attack, or else a potentially winning material advantage (such as an extra Pawn or two).

56. Can you give me some examples of how "sacrificing the exchange" works?

Two illustrations of sound, clear-cut exchange sacrifices follow in Diagrams 79 through 82:

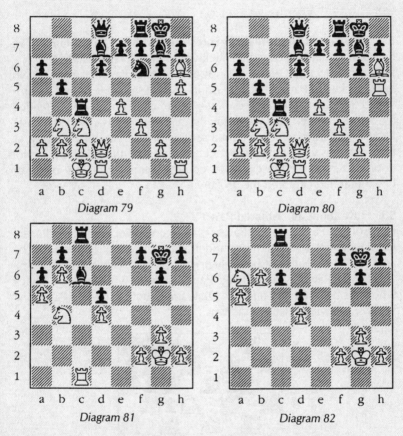

Diagram 79   Diagram 80

Diagram 81   Diagram 82

Diagram 79 shows an example of castling on opposite sides, with both players attacking the other's King. Black is on the move and decides to capture White's *h* Pawn by 1. ... Nxh5. Is this correct?

No! Because after 1. ... Nxh5?, White sacrifices the exchange with 2. Rxh5!, winning a piece (Diagram 80). (If Black recaptures with 2. ... gxh5??, White has 3. Qg5!, pinning Black's Bishop, forcing mate on the next move. White's Queen would capture Black's Bishop,

Qxg7++, and the Queen is protected by the Bishop on h6. Play this out if it is still unclear to you.)

In the second example (Diagram 81), White decides to sacrifice the exchange by 1. Rxc6! bxc6 (forced, for if 1. ... Rxc6 2. Nxc6 bxc6 3. b7 and White will get a new Queen) 2. Nxa6, also getting a Pawn for the exchange. Is this (Diagram 82) good for White?

Definitely! Black has no way of stopping the *b* Pawn from Queening, except by giving up his Rook in two moves, and then he would be lost anyway.

57. What about all those odd expressions in chess? For instance, I've heard of something called a "backward Pawn." What is this?

In Diagram 15 (see Question 31, above), Black's Pawn on c6 is known as a "backward Pawn" because on its current square it cannot be protected from attack by another Black Pawn, and can only be defended by pieces. While "backward Pawns" are not necessarily bad, those, like the c6 Pawn, which are on a *semiopen file*,[4] can be a liability, as they may be vulnerable to attack. Notice that the d5 Pawn is *not* unprotected, since the c6 Pawn could capture an enemy piece or Pawn that had captured the d5 Pawn.

58. How about an "isolated Pawn"?

An "isolated Pawn" has no Pawns of the same color on either adjacent file. Therefore, when it comes under attack, it cannot be defended by another Pawn, but must be protected by pieces. As in the case with a "backward Pawn," an "isolated Pawn" is more vulnerable to attack when it is on a semiopen file. In Diagram 83 both White's *d* Pawn and Black's *a* Pawn are isolated Pawns.

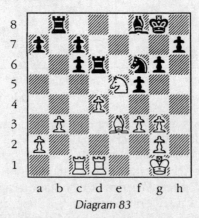

Diagram 83

4. An *open file* is one with no Pawns remaining on it. A *semiopen* file is a file with Pawns of only one color still on it.

A well-known saying in chess literature is "the weakness of an isolated Pawn is not so much in itself, but in the square in front of it." This is because enemy pieces can blockade and/or attack an isolated Pawn from the square in front of it, and they cannot be chased away by Pawns on adjacent files.

59. What is a "doubled Pawn"?
A "doubled Pawn" is two Pawns of the same color on the same file. This can only occur as the result of a Pawn capture earlier. In Diagram 83 White's *g* Pawns and Black's *c* Pawns are doubled Pawns. Incidentally, Black's *c* Pawns are "*isolated* doubled Pawns," and, as they are on a semiopen file, are quite vulnerable to attack. Generally, isolated doubled Pawns are considered a serious weakness.

60. What is a "hole"?
A "hole" is an important square, usually in the center, that cannot be protected from enemy occupation by any of your Pawns. In Diagram 83, the square e5 is a serious "hole" in Black's position, powerfully occupied by White's Knight (which is putting pressure on many squares in Black's position, especially c6, the front Pawn of Black's weak doubled Pawns). Notice that the corresponding square in White's position, e4, is defended from occupation by any Black pieces by the White Pawn on f3.

61. What is a "fianchetto"?
The *fianchetto* ("small flank" in Italian) is a means of developing Bishops on their respective *long diagonals* (these are the a1–h8 and h1–a8 diagonals). To fianchetto a Bishop early in the game, you would move either your *b* or *g* Pawn one or two squares (usually one), and then put your Bishop on the square just vacated, usually on the next move. If White and Black each fianchettoed both Bishops during the same game, their Bishops would, respectively, be on b2, g2, b7 and g7.

62. What does a fianchetto look like?
Here are two standard positions with fianchettoed Bishops:

In the position in Diagram 84 both sides have fianchettoed their White-squared Bishops. This is from an opening (*openings* will be discussed in the next question) called the *Queen's Indian Defense*. Each side hopes to use his fianchettoed Bishop to help fight for control of the important central squares e4 and d5.

In Diagram 85 only Black has fianchettoed a Bishop—on the Kingside—and he hopes to use it to help fight for control of the important

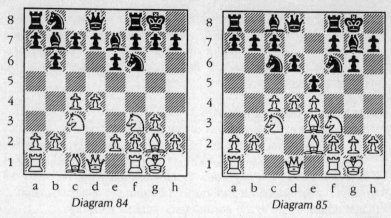

Diagram 84   Diagram 85

central squares e5 and d4. This position is from an opening called the *King's Indian Defense.*

63. What is the "opening"?

The opening, as the term implies, is the beginning stage of the game of chess. It is here that you move some Pawns—usually center Pawns—to make way for the development of your pieces. Several pieces are brought out for both attacking and defensive purposes, and usually castling takes place during this phase. The opening takes roughly ten to fifteen moves on each side. *The opening begins the battle for control of the central squares, which is really what the game of chess is all about* (aside from, of course, checkmating the King). The most important central squares are e4, e5, d4 and d5, although the adjacent squares f4, f5, c4 and c5 are almost as important. Your goals in the opening are basically to develop your minor pieces towards the center, to try to gain at least an equal foothold in control of the center with your Pawns and pieces, and to tuck your King away safely by castling on the appropriate side (depending on the requirements of your position).

Of course, if you blunder badly in the opening you will not survive this initial phase at all. Such early losses always mean you have foolishly invited an attack on your King, or have blindly ignored your opponent's threats by not paying attention to the motive behind his moves.

64. What is an example of a bad mistake in the opening?

Here is an example of encouraging your opponent to attack your weakened position:

Examine the position in Diagram 86. First White plays the bad

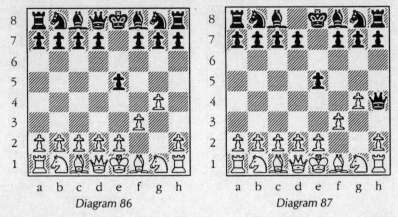

Diagram 86   Diagram 87

opening move 1. f3, to which Black reasonably replies 1. ... e5. 1. f3 is a weak opening move because it does not contribute to helping the development of White's pieces, and only marginally contributes to controlling important central squares. Also, the square f2 for White, and correspondingly f7 for Black, are the most vulnerable during the opening because they are the only squares protected solely by the King.

Now White plays the illogical move 2. g4??, contributing nothing toward development or central control. Even worse, it weakens the square f2 by opening a diagonal, which cannot be contested (to *contest* a diagonal means to attempt to gain control over it), directly to White's King. Not surprisingly, Black responds with 2. ... Qh4++ mate! (Diagram 87.) This debacle, which can also result from White's playing 1. f4 followed by 2. g4??, is known as the "Fool's Mate."

65. Is there any other opening blunder I should especially avoid?
Yes. Here is an example of what has become known as "the bane of beginners," the "Scholar's Mate."

After the opening moves 1. e4 e5 2. Bc4 Bc5 (2. ... Nf6 would be stronger, immediately attacking White's *e* Pawn, though the move played is not actually bad) 3. Qh5, Black sees he is being confronted by a dangerous, albeit premature attack by White (Diagram 88). Unfortunately, Black notices only that White's Queen is now attacking his undefended *e* Pawn, and plays 3. ... Nc6??. At first this appears a good move, as it both protects the *e* Pawn and develops a piece. Unfortunately, it also allows 4. Qxf7++ mate (Diagram 89)!

What went wrong here? Basically, Black didn't recognize that 3. Qh5 contained a dual threat. White's Queen was attacking not only the *e* Pawn, but also, for the second time, the *f* Pawn on the vulnera-

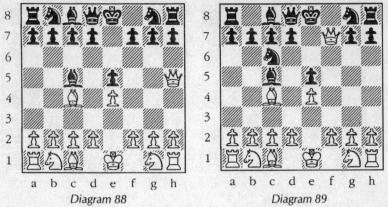

Diagram 88   *Diagram 89*

ble f7 square. Black simply overlooked that White's Bishop on c4 was already hitting at f7, and so after 3. Qh5, White was attacking f7 twice, while Black was defending it once. If Black had seen the full purpose of 3. Qh5, he could have found the forced reply 3. ... Qe7, an excellent defensive move, which protects e5 and f7 simultaneously, while developing a major piece.

The move 3. ... Qe7 also exposes the downside of White's having put his Queen on h5, where, if Black responds correctly, it is not well placed. In fact, if Black does play correctly, he will soon gain a move on White by attacking White's misplaced Queen with 4. ... Nf6. This is called winning a tempo. Literally, you are winning an extra developing move whenever bringing out one of your pieces also drives away one of your opponent's already developed pieces. Usually "long" Queen moves early in the opening are a mistake because almost always your Queen will be driven away by one of your opponent's pieces or Pawns, with a gain of tempo for him. So, objectively, trying to trick your opponent into a "Scholar's Mate" is, in fact, poor opening play, and only works against very inexperienced players.

66. Are there any other notable opening mistakes often made by beginners?

Another, similar sequence of moves, also leading to a "Scholar's Mate," which is very common in games between children, is 1. e4 e5 2. Qh5 Nc6 3. Bc4 Nf6?? 4. Qxf7++ mate. Younger players seem to have an inordinate fondness for moving the "powerful" Queen and "funny" Knight too often. In the catastrophe just described, after White made the dubious aggressive move 2. Qh5, Black correctly defended his e Pawn, but didn't pay attention to the reason behind White's 3. Bc4, as he was too eager to attack White's Queen with his Knight (3. ... Nf6??). Just as in our earlier example, Black's correct reply was

3. ... Qe7. With this move, he would have defended f7, prepared to drive White's Queen away with 4. ... Nf6, and gained a tempo.

67. Do I need to know more about chess openings?

Chess openings, both good and bad, have been almost totally codified; many have acquired exotic names over the centuries such as the *Ruy Lopez* (1. e4 e5 2. Nf3 Nc6 3. Bb5), *Sicilian Defense* (1. e4 c5), *Scotch Game* (1. e4 e5 2. Nf3 Nc6 3. d4 exd4 4. Nxd4), *French Defense* (1. e4 e6 2. d4 d5), *Queen's Gambit* (1. d4 d5 2. c4), *English Opening* (1. c4) and many, many more.

Nevertheless, when you first take up chess it is much more important to learn the principles behind correct opening play than to memorize some opening theory out of a book. Later, after you have played many practice games, and (hopefully!) studied many well-annotated master games in books and/or periodicals, you will discover which openings tend to lead to positions you feel comfortable in. Then it will be time to study some specific openings. After "beginner's books," there are more "opening books" than any other type of chess literature.

68. What is a "gambit"?

A gambit is an opening where one of the players gives up material, usually a Pawn, in the hopes of gaining positional compensation. This compensation usually takes the form of better, faster development and more control of the center. A "sound" gambit often leads to an enduring initiative, that is, an opening advantage that is sustained. Even "unsound" gambits can be difficult for the opponent to handle and require great care in defense.

69. What are some good gambits?

Two gambits still considered to be sound, or at least "unclear" (that is, their soundness or unsoundness has not been decided upon by chess theoreticians) and interesting are:

King's Gambit: 1. e4 e5 2. f4 exf4 3. Nf3 d6 4. d4 g5.
While White controls more of the center, Black has a Pawn more. The King's Gambit can be "declined" (i.e., defended against) by 2. ... Bc5 3. Nf3 d6. (3. fxe4?? would be awful because of 3. ... Qh4+ 4. g3 [forced] Qxe4+, attacking and, because White must move his King out of check, then winning a Rook.)

Smith-Morra Gambit:[5] 1. e4 c5 2. d4 cxd4 3. c3 dxc3 4. Nxc3 Nc6 5. Nf3 d6 6. Bc4 e6 7. 0-0 Nf6 8. Qe2 Be7 9. Rd1 ... .

---

5. Named after the American master Ken Smith and the French master Pierre Morra, both of whom played the gambit often, helping to make it popular.

This is a typical sequence in this modern gambit against the Sicilian Defense. For the Pawn that White sacrifices (3. ... dxc3), he gains more aggressively developed pieces and more space, and is able to place pressure on the d6 Pawn.

This gambit is very popular with players below the master level. Most masters would rather take Black's position, defend carefully and hope to make the extra Pawn tell in the endgame. (More on the "endgame" in Question 72.)

70. What is the "middlegame"?

The middlegame is that part of the game which begins after the opening. There is no clear-cut dividing line between the two phases. But the middlegame is the most complicated part of the game of chess—the part in which most, if not all, of the large-scale fighting takes place. The whole board may be the scene of the struggle, with every piece taking part, and with, occasionally, several local battles going on simultaneously. It is the stage of planning and execution, of attack and defense, of trap and threat, of capture and exchange, of strategy and tactics, of slow maneuvering and rapid action.

The characteristically dominant piece in the middlegame is the Queen. This piece is the heart and soul of most middlegame attacks, and most significant aspects of middlegame complications. The middlegame is where, by and large, you play your most interesting and creative chess. Along with actual practice, the best way to learn correct middlegame strategy is to study well-annotated games of the great masters. Through trial and error, victory and defeat, they discovered the basic truths about most standard positions, and you have only to carefully play over and study their games to gain similar insights.

71. I hear so much about strategy and tactics. What is the difference between them?

Strategy is the plan you form in a given position to achieve a specific goal. It may be aggressive or defensive, depending upon your analysis of the situation.

Tactics, according to the great chess teacher Luděk Pachman in *Modern Chess Strategy* (Dover, 1971), are the "collection of measures and methods for executing one's strategical plan or thwarting the opponent's. ... To this field belong manoeuvers, combinations and sacrifices, as well as double attack, pinning, discovered check, traps, etc." Strategy, then, is your *general* plan; tactics are your *specific* means of carrying out this plan.

72. What is the "endgame"?

This is the final stage of the game, where the position has usually become greatly simplified by many exchanges of pieces and/or Pawns. By the time the endgame is reached, most of the pieces—and almost always the Queens—have been removed by capture. Most endgames center about the struggle of one player to make a material advantage decisive. (Remember that a material advantage is determined by the relative *value* of your and your opponent's pieces. Study the typical point-value assignments given in Question 53.) Usually this takes the form of trying to Queen a Pawn. It is in the endgame where an extra Pawn (or two) or extra piece is most likely to become a clear, winning advantage. In fact, when you are ahead in material in the middlegame, it is to your advantage to simplify the position. Generally you should then try to "trade down," that is, to attempt to bring about even exchanges of pieces and/or Pawns to achieve a winning endgame.

However, while the endgame is *simplified*, it is not necessarily a *simple* stage. Despite the comparatively slight amount of material on the board, there is room for a great deal of subtle maneuvering and clever finesses that make all the difference between victory and defeat. In fact, endgames are notoriously difficult for beginners, who far too often fail to realize their advantage. At some point you will have to learn some basic endgame technique by studying a specific text on the endgame.

73. What exactly throws beginners off in the endgame?

There are two characteristics of endgames that novices find particularly confusing:

- First, after all this talk about how important it is to protect your King, by "tucking it safely away in a corner," away from the action in the center, in the endgame the King is a fighting piece! That's right, most successful endgame play requires that you activate your King as soon as most of the major pieces, generally the Queens and one pair of Rooks, are gone. Generally, you need your King to help attack your opponent's Pawns and minor pieces; it is often also needed to help shepherd one of your Pawns through to Queen.

- Secondly, after all the harping on how important even a single Pawn is, as it is potentially a new Queen, it is a bit disconcerting to learn that there are many, many endgames which are theoretical draws despite one side being a Pawn ahead! This is why it is essential to study basic endgame theory—so you can learn to win won positions and save difficult ones.

74. Can you give some examples of typical endgames?

The most common endgames you will reach are Rook-and-Pawn endings.[6] These endings are those in which each side has a Rook and one to several Pawns; the next most common endings are where each side has a Rook, a minor piece and one to several Pawns. The possibility of going into a King-and-Pawn ending, although less common, is one that has to be considered and evaluated very frequently. In endgames you are constantly being confronted with the decision as to whether or not to exchange your last remaining piece, so that knowing if you are entering a won, lost or drawn King-and-Pawn ending is obviously quite important.

Although it is way beyond the scope of this book to consider endgame theory in detail, we present in the following diagrams two fundamental King-and-Pawn endings.

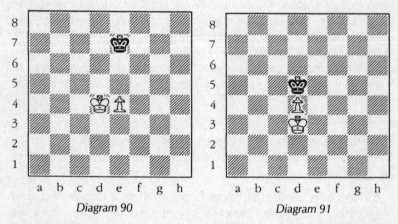

Diagram 90   Diagram 91

Diagram 90: In this position, if White is on the move, he can force a win beginning with 1. Ke5!. This is called *gaining the opposition*. In King-and-Pawn endings, when you are able to force your opponent's King to retreat by moving your King forward, you *have the opposition*. Play might continue 1. ... Ke8 2. Ke6! (gaining control of more squares in front of your Pawn; your goal is for your King to gain control of e8, which is your Queening square) Kd8 3. Kf7! (now you've done it!) Kd7 4. e5 Kd8 5. e6 Kc7 6. e7 ... .(Now Black cannot prevent White from Queening and eventually checkmating him with the new Queen.)

6. Endgames are often referred to as "endings." In contemporary chess literature, "endgame" and "ending" have become almost interchangeable.

46

Diagram 91: This type of position is very common and should be a forced draw. With correct play White should never be able to gain control of his Queening square (d8). If White tries 1. Kc3, then Black must play 1. ... Kd6!, going straight backward, so that after 2. Kc4, he can play 2. ... Kc6!, taking the opposition, preventing the further advance of White's King. White can use only Pawn moves to advance but this will not ultimately help him gain control of d8. After 3. d5+ Kd6, 4. Kd4 Kd7! (going straight backward so as to regain the opposition after . . .) 5. Ke5 Ke7! 6. d6+ Kd7 7. Kd5 Kd8! 8. Kc6 Kc8! (8. Ke6 Ke8! will also draw in the same way) 9. d7+ Kd8. Now the only move that does not lose the Pawn, causing an automatic draw, is 10. Kd6, which is a *stalemate* (see Question 37, above)! This resource of a draw by stalemate is a common defense for the weaker side in many King-and-Pawn endings. If you can learn to calculate correctly whether or not the side with the extra Pawn can gain the opposition, you will win and save many endgames!

75. Since the endgame is so important, could you give some more examples?

Here are two Rook-and-Pawn endings that are as fundamental as the King-and-Pawn endgames we just examined:

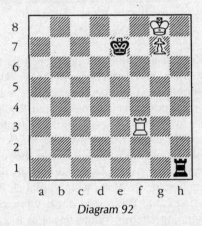

Diagram 92

Diagram 92: This is known as the Lucena position (named after the medieval chess player who wrote about it) and versions of it occur often. As White already controls the Queening square, in this case g8, he has only to drive Black's King a bit farther away, and find a way to evade checks from Black's Rook when he moves his King out from under the cover of the *b* Pawn. This is accomplished by a maneuver called "building a bridge." For example, 1. Re3+ Kd7 (if 1. ... Kf6?? 2.

Kf8!, and White Queens immediately) 2. Re4! Kd6 (any reasonable Rook move for Black, such as 2. ... Rh2, will lead to a similar finale) 3. Kf7 (threatening to win Black's Rook by Queening the Pawn, so Black must start checking) Rf1+ 4. Kg6 Rg1+ 5. Kf6 Rf1+ 6. Kg5! Rg1+ 7. Rg4! (this interposition was the point of 2. Re4!, as now Black can no longer stop White from Queening). Black now resigns, as after 7. ... Rxg4+ 8. Kxg4, with his King three files away, Black can no longer prevent White from Queening. This is also a good example of why it is always a good idea, if you can, to drive the defending side's King as far away from your potential Queening square as possible.

Diagram 93

Diagram 93: Known as Philidor's position, this type of position appears very frequently. It is drawn because the weaker side cannot be forced to give up control of the Queening square, in this case c8. The key to defending such positions is to place your Rook on the rank the enemy King wants to move to, preventing his King from doing so. In this position the only move that draws for Black is 1. ... Rf6!, as White's King is now prevented from going to the sixth rank, which would threaten mate and eventually allow him to drive Black away from the Queening Square. (If White were to play 2. Rh8+, Black simply would go 2. ... Kc7 and White will not have made progress.) The only dangerous winning attempt White now has is 2. c6, after which White would threaten 3. Kb6, as the *c* Pawn would now shield him from Black's Rook (and he would be menacing 4. Rh8++ mate!). However, now that White's Pawn is on the sixth rank, Black can switch over to attack White's King vertically by 2. ... Rf1! In fact, now there is no way for White to escape Black's checks from behind, e.g., 3. Kc5 Rc1+ 4. Kd5 Rd1+, etc. If White moves his King too far away from the *c* Pawn he will lose it to a combined attack by Black's King and Rook. You are urged to try and learn this endgame—you would be surprised how many players never do and keep on losing what are really drawn positions.

One final important fact about most Rook-and-Pawn and King-and-Pawn endgames: having an extra *a* or *h* Pawn (these are commonly called Rook Pawns) seldom leads to a winning position, as it is much easier for the weaker side to retain control of the Queening square with his King. Diagrams 94 and 95 show two examples:

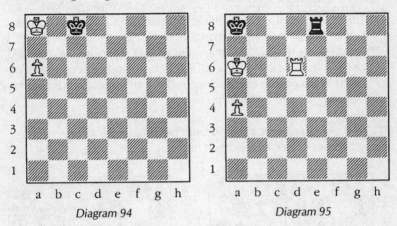

Diagram 94   Diagram 95

In Diagram 94, White's King has been trapped in the corner by Black's! This position is a draw because if Black merely continues to shuttle his King between c7 and c8, White can never get out. Also, if White ever moves his Pawn to a7, it is a stalemate!

The position in Diagram 95 is drawn because Black's King can never be permanently dislodged from the squares a8 or b8 as long as he keeps his Rook on the eighth rank. Without Rooks it is also an easy draw, as White's King can never force Black's away from the Queening square.

76. Would you define a "draw" more precisely?

As in many other games, a draw in chess means that neither side wins or loses. In scored matches, it means that the players will "split the point," because, in chess, you are scored one point for a win, zero for a loss and one-half point for a draw.

77. In general, how does a draw come about?

Draws usually occur for one of the following four reasons:

- Insufficient mating material. When neither side is able to checkmate under any circumstances, such as in King vs. King, or King and Knight vs. King and Bishop, a draw is automatic.

- Mutual agreement. This happens when one player offers the other a draw and the offer is accepted. Proper etiquette under tournament conditions demands that you should first make your move and only then offer a draw. After you have done this you are committed to your draw offer until your opponent either accepts it or rejects it, either verbally or by making his move.
- The "fifty-move rule." After fifty consecutive moves have been played without either a single Pawn moved or piece captured, either side may claim a draw.
- Perpetual check. This means either that, literally, the attacked King cannot escape an endless series of repetitive checks or, were it possible to escape the checks, it still would not be advantageous, or even safe, to do so.

78. Can you give some examples of "perpetual check"?

Two examples of perpetual check follow:

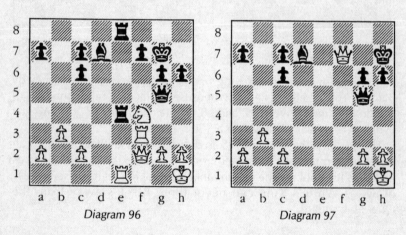

Diagram 96   Diagram 97

The position in Diagram 96 was reached in a game between Alex Sherzer and Roman Dzindzichashvili in their game during the 1992 U.S. Chess Championship. It is White's 25th move, and clearly he appears to be in trouble as he is a Pawn down and facing a fierce Black central initiative. However, Sherzer finds a brilliant drawing combination, beginning with 25. Ne6+!! If Black replies 25. ... Bxe6?, then simply 26. Rxe4 wins the exchange. The reply 25. ... R1xe6?? is likewise refuted by 26. Rxf7+ Kg8 27. Rf8+ Kg7 (or h7) 28. Qf7++ mate! Therefore Black has to play 26. ... R4xe6. Then 27. Rxf7+ Kg8 28. Rf1! R6f7 (forced) 29. Rf8+ Rxf8 (forced, as 29. ... Kg7?? allows 30.

Qf7+! and mate next move!) 30. Qf8+ Kh7 31. Rf7+ Rxf7 32. Qxf7+ drawn (see Diagram 97). This position is a classic, inescapable perpetual check. Black's Queen can check White forever on f7 and f8, while White's King can only shuttle back and forth between h7 and h8.

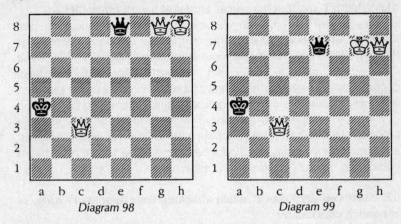

Diagram 98   Diagram 99

The next example is from a game between Paul Brandts and the author, played in the Eastern Championship, New York, 1970. In reply to 84. ... Qe8+, Mr. Brandts, probably somewhat tired after seven consecutive hours of play (!), mistakenly interposed by Queening his Pawn on g7 by 85. g8=Q? (Diagram 98.) Why was this incorrect?

Because after 85. ... Qh5+ 86. Qh7 Qe8+ 87. Kg7 Qe7+! 88. Kh6 Qh4+ 89. Kg6 Qe4+! 90. Kg7 Qe7+ the game was drawn. (Diagram 99.) The position after 87. Kg7 Qe7+ has been repeated and will inevitably be repeated again (in tournament play, you can also claim a draw when you are about to bring about a three-time occurrence of a position). White was caught in an amusing "windmill" of checks, from which he could never escape without giving up his new Queen for nothing. This type of perpetual check, where it is possible, but useless (or sometimes foolish) to evade the checks, is a very common tactic.

79. May I "take back" a move if I change my mind?
No! Unless you are playing against a teacher or a much stronger player, with whom you have previously agreed that it is all right for you to take back moves, you must stand by your decision, wise or unwise, once a piece has been moved.

80. What happens if I find I have made a move I am not allowed to make?
This is an "illegal," that is, impossible or impermissible, move. An ille-

gal move must be retracted and, if possible, a legal move must be made with the piece that was moved. If you cannot make a legal move with the piece you touched first, then you are allowed to make any other legal move available, and there is no penalty.

81. What if I just touch a piece? Do I still have to move it?

Absolutely, yes! You must move a piece if you touch it. One of the best things about chess is that it teaches you to take responsibility for your decisions. Not only must you move any piece you touch, but if you touch one of your opponent's men you must capture it (if it is a legal capture), and, once your hand leaves a piece after you have placed it on a new square, the move is completed and may not be taken back.

The only exception to this rule is if you want to straighten out a crooked piece or have clearly accidentally touched or brushed against a piece. Then you may say *J'adoube* (pronounced jah-DOOB; this is French for "I adjust") and move another piece if you wish.

82. Must you say "check" when attacking your opponent's King, or announce checkmate?

Absolutely not! While it is okay for absolute beginners to make these statements when practicing against each other or a teacher, it is really not required, nor is it even considered polite! It is a good idea to take responsibility for noticing the immediate effects of your opponent's moves as soon as possible.

83. How much time can you take when deciding on making a move?

In serious tournament or match play there is a stipulated time limit, generally known in chess circles as the time control. A player who exceeds the time control loses the game automatically. Nowadays, typical time controls for serious, rated tournament play might be either thirty moves in ninety minutes for each player, or forty moves in two hours each, with twenty-five moves for each player per hour thereafter.

84. Are there variations on this?

Very frequently now there is a second method of time control used called "sudden death," where both players are allowed only one hour each to complete the game.

85. How is the time monitored?

In serious tournament or match play, the time limit or limits are monitored with "chess clocks," which are generally two clocks built into one rectangular frame, with two "start/stop" buttons on the top. When you have completed your move you push the button atop your clock, and your opponent's clock starts. When your opponent replies, he pushes his button and your clock starts again. (Note that a player's clock is running only during his own move.)

86. Are clocks ever used in any other way in chess?
Another very popular form of chess with clocks is called "blitz" or "five-minute" chess. In this type of chess each player has only five minutes in which to make all his moves, i.e., the entire game can take at most ten minutes! This is very popular with quick players who have good intuition.

87. What about an ordinary game with a friend?
Of course, in friendly games without clocks there is no specific time limit, but players should be governed by a sportsmanlike attitude and not take more than a reasonable amount of time for their moves. It really is unfair to try to "outsit" your opponent!

88. Are there any variations on "normal" chess that can be recommended to beginners?
Yes. There is one that I call "mini-chess." In "mini-chess" each side begins the game with a King, six, seven or eight Pawns each, and only one piece—usually a Bishop, Knight or Rook. The idea in "mini-chess" is to become comfortable with Pawn moves and captures, and get plenty of practice using each piece. As you are beginning in an endgame, you are also forced to learn to use your King aggressively. This type of practice, with should begin with the King, Pawns and piece on their original squares, is very useful in learning just how materialistic a game chess really is. In "mini-chess," just as in "normal" chess, you are trying to gain more space, have more effectively developed pieces, perhaps win at least a Pawn (a potential extra Queen!) and then win the game through attrition. When using a Queen in "mini-chess," you may want to combine it with one of the other pieces you have already become comfortable using, so as to introduce the possibility of early attacks against the enemy King.

89. What does a complete, annotated game look like?
The following game was played at the Porz/Koln tournament, held in (West) Germany at the end of 1981. Try playing it out!

Name of opening: QUEEN'S GAMBIT DECLINED (Semi-Slav variation)

White: Anthony Miles		*Black: Dr. Paul Troger*
1.	**d4**	e6

This move allows White the option of playing 2. e4, and, after 2. ... d5, a French Defense would result. However, by his next move Miles shows that he prefers to play a Queen's Gambit.

2.	**c4**	**d5**

The Queen's Gambit is not a genuine gambit, as it is nearly impossible, and very dangerous, for Black to keep the Pawn, if he chooses to capture it on his next move (3. ... dxc4).

3.	**Nc3**	**c6**

White has developed his Queenside Knight to its best square, immediately putting pressure on d5 and e4, and Black has responded by reinforcing his control of d5. For novices, it probably would be better to play 3. ... Nf6 in this standard Queen's Gambit Declined position, with the idea of following this up with 4. ... Be7 and 5. ... 0-0. This would be more in keeping with the wise general principle that encourages speedy development with early castling.

4.	**Bf4**	

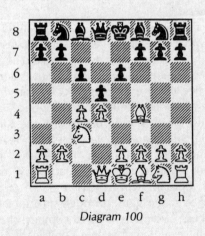

Diagram 100

Now see Diagram 100. This move is slightly unusual, 4. Nf3 and 4. e3 being more common, although 4. Bf4 is also a perfectly reasonable developing move ... and it provokes Black into a careless response.

4.	**...**	**Bd6?**

Apparently reasonable, but superficially thought out. It seems like a good idea for Black to attempt to trade off one of White's developed men by developing one of his own. In this case, however, after the exchange of Bishops, Black's Queen is left on a more vulnerable square than before. Also, the move played does nothing to combat White's strategic plan in this position, that of central expansion by moving his *e* Pawn to e4. It was still not too late for Black instead to play 4. ... Nf6, hindering, for the time being, White's central activity and preparing to play the solid, further-developing move 5. ... Be7, probably followed by 6. ... 0-0.

| 5. | **Bxd6** | **Qxd6** |
| 6. | **e4** | **dxe4?** |

Diagram 101

(See Diagram 101.) Here, Black has made another mistake. He probably thought that after 7. Nxe4? Qb4+, White would be forced to defend with 8. Qd2 (otherwise White would lose his *b* Pawn) Qxd2+ 9. Nxd2, resulting in an *equal position.*[7] However, it is wrong to assume that all recaptures are automatic. Furthermore, in this position, White has a remarkable resource:

| 7. | **c5!** |

This *zwischenzug* (literally, an "in-between move") is what Black overlooked. Rather than recapturing on e4, White attacks Black's Queen and prevents it from going to b4, even driving it backwards! If Black now should try 7. ... Qf4 to defend the *e* Pawn, then by 8. Nge2 Qf5 9. Ng3, White would win back the Pawn and subsequently force

7. An *equal position*, or *even game*, describes a situation in which, objectively, both sides have equal chances, that is, neither player has an advantage. The expression *equal position* does *not* refer to the position of the pieces of either player alone.

In chess literature, achieving an equal position is often referred to as *equalizing*, or gaining *equality*. Equality does not mean that the game must end in a draw, but only that the players have even chances.

Black to lose the right to castle. In the game, White accomplishes these ends anyhow, by the following:

7.	...	Qe7
8.	Nxe4	Nf6

Black's last move was his best try in an already difficult situation. He hopes that White will either trade off his powerful Knight on e4 or at least let Black castle. White, however, correctly plays:

9.	Nd6+	Kd8

Diagram 102

Take a good look at Black's miserable position after 9. ... Kd8 (Diagram 102). *This is exactly the kind of situation you are trying to avoid in the opening.* Black's King has lost the right to castle and is trapped in the center. Black's pieces are cramped and will be difficult to develop. Conversely, White has much more maneuvering space, controls more of the important center squares and will soon be able to castle. He will thus put his King in a safe position and also "connect" his Rooks, which will be mobilized much sooner than Black's. White therefore already has a "strategically won" game. But White's game will not "win itself"! White must still finish his development, form a sensible plan for opening lines against Black's King, and execute it carefully. The rest of this game provides a good example of how White can exploit his advantages.

10.	Nf3	Ne8

White develops his other Knight to its best square, while Black tries to trade off the "bone in his throat," the Knight on d6.

11.	Nc4!	

An excellent move! Black is seeking relief through exchanges, so it is to White's advantage to keep as many pieces on the board as he can to use in the coming attack on Black's King.

| 11. | . . . | b5 |

If Black instead played 11. ... b6, trying to break White's stranglehold on the dark squares d6 and e5, then 12. Bd3! bxc5 13. dxc5 Qxc5 14. 0-0. Now White could quickly develop a powerful attack against the exposed Black King, particularly by bringing one of his Rooks to the now open *d* file. It is pretty much a good bet that if you have developed three pieces and castled, against an opponent who has only brought out his Queen, as in this possible variation, you have made a sound Pawn sacrifice!

| 12. | Na5! | |

While normally it is not a good idea to place a Knight on the edge of the board, where it will command fewer squares, here this is a fine move, putting pressure on the weak c6 Pawn and helping to keep Black cramped.

By the way, why didn't White capture Black's *b* Pawn *en passant* on his last move? In the variation 12. cxb6 axb6 13. Nxb6, doesn't White win a Pawn? Answer: No, because after 13. ... Qb4+!, simultaneously attacking White's King and his Knight on b6, Black wins a piece! This tactical maneuver is called a *double attack*.

12.	. . .	Qc7
13.	Qd2	Nd7
14.	Ne5!	

How is this possible? Can't Black capture twice on e5 (that is, capture on e5 for two successive moves), winning the *e* Pawn?

| 14. | . . . | Nxe5? |

Another mistake. Black would have been better off playing the horribly passive-looking 14. ... Nb8, which would allow him to defend f7 with his Queen, while reinforcing the defense of c6. Play might have proceeded 15. Be2 f6 16. Nf3. White would then still have to castle and bring his Rooks to the center to continue his attack. Of course, this position would be hopeless also. Now, however, after 14. ... Nxe5?, White does not even have to castle to get a winning attack.

| 15. | dxe5+ | Ke7 |
| | (discovered check!) | |

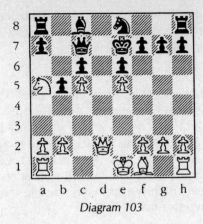

Diagram 103

(See Diagram 103.) This is called a *discovered check* because checking is brought about by *clearing the path* between White's Queen and Black's King. Actually, I am sure Black realized he couldn't win White's *e* Pawn because of the discovered check, and probably thought that, from this position, he could escape from the center with his King via f8, and fight on. However, White has an amazing tactic available to him now, based upon his overwhelming control of the d6 square. Do you see it?

| 16. | | **Qd6+!!** |

An impossible-looking move, but it is, in fact, only a sham Queen sacrifice. If 16. ... Nxd6?, White would simply play 17. e(or c)xd6+, forking Black's King and Queen. Black would have to give back the Queen for two Pawns and enter a lost endgame, where his extra two Pawns would be insufficient compensation for being a Knight down.

16.	...	**Qxd6**
17.	**cxd6+**	**Kd7**
18.	**Rc1**	**f6**

White's consistent play in this game is bearing fruit. By recapturing the Queen with his *c* Pawn, White has made the weak c6 Pawn an undefendable target. Black's last move is an attempt to break up White's strong center. But, as the *c* Pawn will not "run away," White reinforces his center before taking the *c* Pawn.

| 19. | **f4** | **g5** |

The best try in a lost position. If White were to play 20. fxg5, Black would have 20. ... fxe5, breaking up White's central Pawn chain and giving him some fighting chances.

| 20. | g3 | gxf4 |
| 21. | Bg2! | |

Another nice sham sacrifice, as 21. ... fxg3?? would allow 22. Bxc6+, with White winning a Rook. Black's actual next move saves his Rook on a8, but his game has become hopeless.

| 21. | ... | Rb8 |
| 22. | Bxc6+ | Kd8 |

Diagram 104

(See Diagram 104.) Now, simply 23. gxf4 would give White a winning, Pawn-up endgame, but he has a much stronger, sharper move. Do you see it?

| 23. | d7! | Bxd7 |

This is forced, as White is forking Black's Bishop and Knight with his Pawn on d7, and so Black must capture it or lose a piece.

| 24. | Rd1 | Resigns. |

Black cannot defend the pinned Bishop on d7. After, for example, 24. ... fxg3 25. Rxd7+ Kc8 26. hxg3, White would be a piece ahead with a continuing attack. In this probable variation White would very shortly win either Black's *a* or *h* Pawn, while Black's remaining pieces would be virtually paralyzed. Masters almost always resign in such hopeless positions. Miles has played the most consistently logical moves throughout, letting none of his opponent's errors go unpunished.

90. You say that if I want to enjoy the older chess books, I need to

know "descriptive" chess notation. How is descriptive notation different from algebraic notation?

In descriptive notation, each file is named for the piece that stands on it at the beginning of the game. The name remains constant, even after the pieces have moved away from their original squares. Thus, the file on which the Kings stand in the original position (see Diagram 1, at the beginning of this book, showing the "initial position") is known as the "King file." The file on which the Queens stand is known as the "Queen file." The file on which the Queen Bishops (that is, the Bishops next to the Queens) stand is called the "Queen Bishop file." The file on which the King Rooks (the Rooks on the Kingside) stand is called the "King Rook file." To translate: in algebraic notation the King Bishop file, for example, would be the *f* file and the Queen Knight file would be the *b* file. (Older books tend to follow English grammar more strictly, talking of the "King's file," the "Queen's Bishop's file" and so forth. I have followed the more recent, and more abbreviated, practice here.)

In descriptive, the Pawns are named for the file they stand on. Thus, starting from the *a* file and moving right (or left, from Black's point of view), we have the "Queen Rook Pawn," "Queen Knight Pawn," "Queen Bishop Pawn," "Queen Pawn," "King Pawn," "King Bishop Pawn," "King Knight Pawn" and "King Rook Pawn." When a Pawn captures, it changes its file, and consequently its name. Also, as already suggested, in descriptive notation the pieces are often referred to based on the side they begin on, as in calling the Rook starting on a1 the "Queen Rook" (QR), the Knight on b1 the "Queen Knight" (QKt or QN), the Bishop beginning on f1 the "King Bishop" (KB), etc.

In descriptive notation "check" is usually abbreviated as "ch," rather than the "+" of algebraic. Also, an en passant capture is usually followed by the initials "e.p."

91. Is there anything about descriptive notation that might be confusing?

In descriptive notation the ranks are numbered 1 through 8, as they are in algebraic, but *which* rank has *which* number depends on whether you are looking from White's point of view or Black's! Thus, in descriptive notation the square the White King starts out on is called "King 1" (abbreviated to K1). From Black's point of view, however, if later in the game he occupied that same square, he would call it K8. The heart of this system is that each square has *two identities*, depending on whose side you are viewing it from. Diagram 105 identifies each square both from White's perspective *and* from Black's.

QR1 / QR8	QKt1 / QKt8	QB1 / QB8	Q1 / Q8	K1 / K8	KB1 / KB8	KKt1 / KKt8	KR1 / KR8
QR2 / QR7	QKt2 / QKt7	QB2 / QB7	Q2 / Q7	K2 / K7	KB2 / KB7	KKt2 / KKt7	KR2 / KR7
QR3 / QR6	QKt3 / QKt6	QB3 / QB6	Q3 / Q6	K3 / K6	KB3 / KB6	KKt3 / KKt6	KR3 / KR6
QR4 / QR5	QKt4 / QKt5	QB4 / QB5	Q4 / Q5	K4 / K5	KB4 / KB5	KKt4 / KKt5	KR4 / KR5
QR5 / QR4	QKt5 / QKt4	QB5 / QB4	Q5 / Q4	K5 / K4	KB5 / KB4	KKt5 / KKt4	KR5 / KR4
QR6 / QR3	QKt6 / QKt3	QB6 / QB3	Q6 / Q3	K6 / K3	KB6 / KB3	KKt6 / KKt3	KR6 / KR3
QR7 / QR2	QKt7 / QKt2	QB7 / QB2	Q7 / Q2	K7 / K2	KB7 / KB2	KKt7 / KKt2	KR7 / KR2
QR8 / QR1	QKt8 / QKt1	QB8 / QB1	Q8 / Q1	K8 / K1	KB8 / KB1	KKt8 / KKt1	KR8 / KR1

Diagram 105

92. Has descriptive notation always been the same?

No. From about the middle of the 19th century until the early 1960's the Knight was designated by the symbol "Kt." From about 1960 onwards, most descriptive texts changed to using "N" for Knight, as in the algebraic literature.

93. Can you give me any tips for learning descriptive notation?

It is probably a good idea to review how all the files would be referred to in descriptive notation. In descriptive, the *a* through *h* files would be called, in abbreviated form, the QR, QKt, QB, Q, K, KB, KKt and KR files respectively.

Descriptive notation is logical if you just remember that each square has a double designation. Suppose White starts the game by advancing his King Pawn two squares. We would write this move as "1. P-K4." If Black replied by also moving his King Pawn two squares, we would write *his* move as "1. ... P-K4." Obviously, in this notation it is essential to know at all times if a Black or White move is being referred to. Below follows an example of a well-known opening trap, written in descriptive notation, with the same moves given in algebraic in parentheses:

PHILIDOR'S DEFENSE

	White	Black
1.	P-K4 (e4)	P-K4 (e5)
2.	Kt-KB3 (Nf3)	P-Q3 (d6)
3.	B-QB4 (Bc4)	B-KKt5 (Bg4)
4.	Kt-QB3 (Nc3)	P-KR3? (h6?)

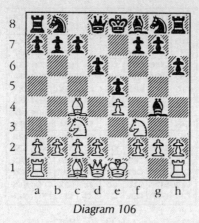

Diagram 106

(See Diagram 106.) Black's last move is a careless blunder, which is punished dramatically.

5.	**Kt × KP! (Nxe5!)**	**B × Q?? (Bxd1??)**

Another bad blunder. Black should have played 5. ... P × Kt (dxe5). He then would have acquiesced in the loss of a Pawn and given White a powerful attacking position, but that was better than what follows.

6.	**B × P ch (Bxf7+)**	**K-K2 (Ke7)**
7.	**Kt-Q5 mate! (N-d5++)**	

Another cautionary tale about the potential weakness, early in the game, of the KB2 (f2 and f7) squares!

Much of the chess literature in English refers to both forms of chess notation, especially books about openings, where references to "King Pawn" and "Queen Pawn" openings abound. In order for you to be able to study and enjoy the vast bulk of classic English and American chess literature, you must learn descriptive notation, as most of the greatest works are still available only in descriptive. When you read the "Suggestions for Further Reading" at the end of this book, you will find that at least half of the titles recommended for reading are in descriptive notation.

94. In descriptive notation, if both pieces of the same type can move to the same square, how can you tell which one is being moved?
When you can move more than one Rook, Knight or Queen (remember, you can have more than one Queen!) to the same square, you indicate this by writing a "/" after the abbreviation for the piece moved, and then the square from which it is moved. In Diagram 107,

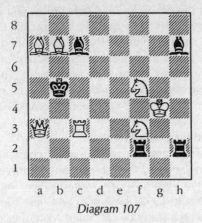
Diagram 107

if it is White's move, he can play 1. R-Kt3 ch, or 1. Q-Kt3 ch, but either 1. Kt/3-Q4 mate or 1. Kt/5-Q4 mate would be better! As both Knights are on the King Bishop file, you need to state only which *rank* the Knight you are moving is on.

Now, supposing that it is Black's move in the above position, what would you, as Black, do? Answer: 1. ... R/B7-Kt7 ch 2. Kt-Kt3 (forced) R × Kt checkmate! "R/B7" distinguishes the Rook on the Bishop file from the one on the Rook file (written as "R/R7").

95. Is there a major American chess organization, and are there any major national American chess periodicals?

The United States Chess Federation, usually called the "USCF," is the official national American chess organization. The USCF has over 70,000 paid members and publishes the leading American chess magazine, *Chess Life*, issued monthly. To play in serious amateur (or professional) chess tournaments in the U.S., you must become a USCF member, as they provide the official ratings for all such U.S. events. Membership in the USCF includes a subscription to *Chess Life*—a superb periodical that provides material for both novice and master alike.

The USCF also provides a great deal of support for scholastic chess and publishes *School Mates*, a bimonthly magazine for beginning young chess players. For information about the USCF and its publications, you are encouraged to write to: U.S. Chess, 186 Route 9W, New Windsor, NY 12553.

96. Are there any other major chess periodicals I might be interested in?

Certainly. Another excellent American chess periodical is *Inside*

Chess, published biweekly. *Inside Chess* brings you the latest games, news and commentaries very quickly, as you get 26 issues a year. Although aimed more at intermediate to advanced players than at beginners, *Inside Chess* frequently contains superb articles on tactics by Nikolay Minev and on opening theory by John Donaldson. Subscription information about *Inside Chess* can be obtained by writing to: I.C.E., Inc., P.O. Box 19457, Seattle, WA 98109.

97. Is chess good for children?

Absolutely, yes! The Russians, who elevated chess to a national pastime, have always believed that chess study improves math and verbal skills and have vigorously promoted chess instruction in their elementary schools. In 1992, the American Chess Foundation (in New York City) sponsored a study by Dr. Stuart Margulies on "The Effect of Chess on Reading Scores." Dr. Margulies conducted his study in Public School District 9, in the South Bronx, a New York inner-city neighborhood. Basically the results were that chess does improve children's reading scores, and that teachers in District 9 believed "that chess-playing students develop enhanced ego strength as they increase their chess competence." According to Dr. Margulies, "The cognition processes [in chess and reading] are very similar. Both reading and chess are decision-making activities and some transfer of training from one to the other may be expected."

98. What can you really get out of chess?

Besides the competitive excitement of winning and losing, of taking the intellectual risk of being fully responsible for your actions whatever happens, there is to my mind, first and foremost, creative satisfaction. Consider the positions in Diagrams 108 and 109.

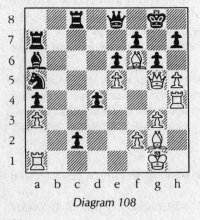

Diagram 108

Diagram 109

In each of the following two positions, White has the opportunity to create a beautiful mating combination (that is, a combination that results in mate), involving heavy sacrifices. First try to figure them out yourself, then study the answers below:

Diagram 108: White seems to have a powerful attack going, but it looks difficult to break through, and Black has those dangerous passed c and d Pawns. White plays 1. Qh6!, and Black hurries to play 1. ... Qf8, offering to trade Queens, breaking up the attack. White then plays the surprising 2. Qxh7+!! Kxh7 3. hxg+ (discovered, double check) Kxg6 4. Be4++ mate!

Diagram 109: Black's position seems a little cramped but solid enough at first glance. Still, aren't a lot of White's pieces pointing at Black's Kingside, while most of Black's men are on the Queenside? Yes indeed, for White finds 1. Nh6+! (a beautiful "line opening" sacrifice, prying open the a1–h8 diagonal) gxh6 2. Rxc6!!. Now, when Black realizes that any recapture on c6 would allow 3. Qd4, with an unstoppable mate on h8 next move, Black resigns.

Now, which of these two positions was played by the former World Chess Champion Bobby Fischer, against L. Miagmasuren at the Sousse Interzonal Tournament of 1967, and which was played by the author's friend, the strong amateur Steven Anderson, at the National Chess Congress, held in Philadelphia, 1993? You can't tell, can you? That is because they are both attractive combinations, and although Fischer played the one in Diagram 108, I am sure he would have been equally proud to have played the one in Diagram 109.

My point is that while not anyone can hit a 450-foot home run, or throw a 70-yard touchdown pass, most of us can get good enough at chess to play a well-thought-out game, or create a beautiful combination, which we can save (by recording it) and enjoy.

99. What must you specifically do to get good at chess?

Study and practice. There is no way around it. You must play a lot of games both against your peers and, preferably, against people somewhat stronger than you. You must also study well-annotated games of the great masters. This way, knowing what correct, creative chess playing looks like becomes a form of pattern recognition that you will eventually apply automatically. Then, if you ever get to the point where you enjoy playing over and trying to understand fine games, I guarantee that your understanding *and* your playing strength will improve.

You should also, especially at the beginning, study tactics, by going through and attempting to solve collections of combinations, because tactics are the basic, unique language of chess. You create winning positions with good strategy, and usually resolve them with good tactics.

100. Should I learn to play chess if I can't stand to lose?

No! You will have to lose hundreds, most likely thousands, of games before you get any good—it is part of the learning process. Besides, you usually learn more from your defeats than your victories. I encourage you to record your more serious (slow) games—both wins and losses—to study later, when your mind is fresh. Remember that a hard-fought draw, or even a well-contested, exciting loss, can still be satisfying if it contributes to a greater understanding of the game.

101. What is the best reason for learning chess?

I don't know. But my personal favorite is:

> On the Chess-board lies and hypocrisy do not survive long. The creative combination lays bare the presumption of a lie; the merciless fact, culminating in a checkmate, contradicts the hypocrite. Our little Chess is one of the sanctuaries, where this principle of justice has occasionally had to hide to gain sustenance and a respite, after the army of mediocrities had driven it from the market-place.
>
> —Emanuel Lasker (World Chess Champion, 1894–1921),
>   in *Lasker's Manual of Chess*, 1932.

Suggestions for Further Reading

The following list is in no way intended to be all-inclusive. In fact, I could easily have included more than *twice as many* very worthwhile English-language chess titles! I have attempted to list all the generally recognized instructional chess classics in English, with a healthy selection of books I have personally found to be both instructive and entertaining. I have included hardly any specific books on chess openings. While there are always many good ones in print, they tend to have a somewhat transitory value, as opening theory is constantly changing.

After each description, I have placed my evaluation as to what level of player—beginner, intermediate or advanced—will benefit most from that book. Also, I have indicated whether the book uses algebraic or descriptive chess notation.

1. Adams, Jimmy, editor and translator. **Mikhail Chigorin: The Creative Chess Genius.** Caissa Editions, 1987. A superbly researched biography of Russia's greatest 19th-century player, with 100 deeply annotated games. Advanced. Algebraic.
2. Agur, Elie. **Bobby Fischer: A Study of His Approach to Chess.** Cadogan Press, 1992. A profound study of the middlegame, using generally lesser-known Fischer games. Advanced. Algebraic.
3. Alekhine, Alexander. **My Best Games of Chess 1908–1937.** Two volumes in one. G. Bell & Sons Ltd., 1927 and 1939; reprinted Dover, 1992. Perhaps the most exciting and instructive autobiographical games collection ever published. Intermediate–advanced. Descriptive.
4. ———. **On the Road to the World Championship.** Pergamon Press, 1984. Has the best annotations to his epochal world-championship match against Capablanca. Advanced. Algebraic.
5. Botvinnik, M. M. **Botvinnik: One Hundred Selected Games.** MacGibbon & Kee, 195l; reprinted Dover, 1960. Thorough, demanding, instructive annotations of his best games by the first Soviet world chess champion. Advanced. Descriptive.
6. Bronstein, David. **200 Open Games.** B. T. Batsford, Ltd., 1973; reprinted Dover, 1991. A great grandmaster's entire praxis with double King–Pawn (1. e4 e5) openings. Intermediate. Descriptive.
7. ———. **Zurich International Chess Tournament 1953.** Translated from the Russian by Jim Marfia. Dover, 1979. Bronstein spent three years analyzing all the games from what many still consider to be the strongest tournament ever held. A masterpiece and a virtual textbook on the middlegame. Advanced. Algebraic.
8. Capablanca, J. R. **My Chess Career.** Macmillan Co., 1920; reprinted Dover, 1969. Confident, clear, even arrogant notes to the best early games of a chess genius. Intermediate–advanced. Descriptive.
9. Chernev, Irving. **Capablanca's Best Chess Endings: 60 Complete Games.** Oxford, 1978; reprinted Dover, 1982. Endgames both enjoyable and exciting! Intermediate–advanced. Algebraic.
10. ———. **Logical Chess, Move by Move.** Simon & Schuster, 1957. A superb elementary work, explaining *every move* of the well-chosen illustrative games. Beginner. Descriptive.

11. ———. **The Most Instructive Games of Chess Ever Played: 62 Masterpieces of Chess Strategy.** Simon & Schuster, 1965; reprinted Dover, 1992. A terrific selection of thematic games, lucidly explained. Intermediate. Descriptive.

12. ———, & Kenneth Harkness. **An Invitation to Chess.** Simon & Schuster, 1945. A great elementary text, charmingly written and profusely illustrated with diagrams. Beginner. Descriptive.

13. Clarke, P. H. **Petrosian's Best Games of Chess 1946–63.** G. Bell & Sons Ltd., 1964; reprinted B. T. Batsford, 1992. Perhaps the best attempt at explaining the highly complex style of a great former world champion. Intermediate–advanced. Descriptive.

14. Coles, R. N. **Dynamic Chess: The Modern Style of Aggressive Play.** Sir Isaac Pitman & Sons, Ltd., London, 1956; revised and enlarged edition, Dover, 1966. Excellent analysis of the profound changes in chess strategy caused by first the Hypermodern, and, later, the post-World-War-II Russian school of chess play. Intermediate–advanced. Descriptive.

15. du Mont, J. **The Basis of Combination in Chess.** Routledge, 1938; reprinted Dover, 1978. A great classic, much admired by Alekhine. Will never become dated. Intermediate. Descriptive.

16. Dvoretsky, Mark. **Secrets of Chess Tactics.** B. T. Batsford, 1992. A great modern teacher's insights into combinative positions. Demanding, but worth the effort. Advanced. Algebraic.

17. Euwe, Max, M. Blaine & J. F. S. Rumble. **The Logical Approach to Chess.** Sir Isaac Pitman & Sons, Ltd., 1958; reprinted Dover, 1982. A delightfully clear book for the novice, correctly concentrating on middle- and endgame instruction. Beginner. Descriptive.

18. ———, & David Hooper. **A Guide to Chess Endings.** Corrected edition, Dover, 1976. An excellent, clearly written, concise one-volume work on basic endgame theory. Intermediate–advanced. Descriptive.

19. ———, & H. Kramer. **The Middle Game.** 2 volumes. Book One: Static Features. Book Two: Dynamic and Subjective Features. G. Bell & Sons Ltd., 1964–65. The most elaborate and carefully planned textbook on this obviously vital part of a chess game. Intermediate–advanced. Descriptive.

20. ———, & Walter Meiden. **Chess Master vs. Chess Amateur.** David McKay, 1964; reprinted Dover, 1994. Excellent and instructive examples of a typical novice's errors punished by the correct play of a master. Beginner–intermediate. Descriptive.

21. Evans, Larry. **New Ideas in Chess.** Pitman Publishing Corp., 1958; reprinted Dover, 1994. A modern classic, emphasizing the analysis of positions from the four most important viewpoints: Pawn structure, space, force and time. Beginner–intermediate. Descriptive.

22. ———. **What's the Best Move?** Simon and Schuster, 1973. A sensible, entertaining and instructive textbook in a question-and-answer format. Beginner–intermediate. Descriptive.

23. Fine, Reuben. **Lessons from My Games.** David McKay, 1958; reprinted Dover, 1982. Masterpieces of logic, didactically rendered. Intermediate–advanced. Descriptive.

24. Fischer, Bobby. **My 60 Memorable Games.** With introductions to the games by International Grandmaster Larry Evans. Simon and Schuster, 1969. *The most important chess book written by an American player* and one of the best, and most remorselessly objective, game collections ever published. Intermediate–advanced. Descriptive.

25. ———, Stuart Margulies & Donn Mosenfelder. **Bobby Fischer Teaches Chess.** Basic Systems, 1966; reprinted many, many times by Bantam Books, Inc. The best-selling chess book of all time, with over 1,000,000 copies printed! Beginner, no notation (i.e., all instruction is done with diagrams).

26. Gelfer, Israel. **Positional Chess Handbook.** B. T. Batsford Ltd., 1991. Contains 495 carefully chosen middle- and endgame positions requiring good technique to solve. Intermediate–advanced. Algebraic.

27. Hammond, J., & R. Jamieson. **C. J. S. Purdy: His Lfe, His Games and His Writings.** John Hammond, 1982. A marvelous book, containing generous selections from Purdy's best articles, which demonstrate an uncanny ability to explain difficult chess concepts to average players. Intermediate. Descriptive.

28. Hays, Lou. **Bobby Fischer: Complete Games of the American World Chess Champion.** Condensed annotations by Senior Master John Hall. Hays Publishing, 1992. By far the best collection of all of Fischer's known tournament, match and exhibition games. Superbly indexed. Intermediate–advanced. Algebraic.

29. ———, & John Hall. **Combination Challenge!** Hays Publishing, 1991. A carefully selected, attractively arranged collection of 1,154 combinative positions, grouped by theme. Intermediate–advanced. Algebraic.

30. Heidenfeld, W. **Draw!** Edited, with a Foreword, by John Nunn. George Allen & Unwin, 1982. A terrific, deeply annotated collection of exciting, often famous, *drawn* games. Advanced. Algebraic.

31. Hort, Vlastimil, & Vlastimil Jansa. **The Best Move.** RHM Press, 1980. A carefully conceived, quite demanding, but clearly explicated collection of largely middlegame positions, requiring some hard work to solve. Intermediate–advanced. Algebraic.

32. Karpov, Anatoly. **Chess at the Top: 1979–1984.** Pergamon Press, 1984. The great strategist's own account of his peak period, with superb notes to his best games. Intermediate–advanced. Algebraic.

33. Kasparov, Garry. **The Test of Time.** Pergamon Press, 1986; reprinted with corrections, 1991. The world champion's very best games, with exhaustively thorough annotations. Advanced. Algebraic.

34. Keene, Raymond. **Aron Nimzowitsch: A Reappraisal.** G. Bell & Sons, 1974. An unusually well researched and enthusiastically written biography of the leading Hypermodern player, by our most prolific contemporary chess author. Advanced. Descriptive.

35. Keres, Paul. **Grandmaster of Chess.** 3 volumes (**The Early Years, The Middle Years** and **The Later Years**). Translated and edited by Harry Golembek. Jenkins, 1964, 1966 and 1969. A perennial world-championship candidate, Keres, perhaps more than any other grandmaster, could write engagingly for a wide range of players, speaking to amateur and expert alike. Intermediate–advanced. Descriptive.

36. ———. **Practical Chess Endings.** B. T. Batsford, Ltd., 1984. Probably the best overall one-volume work on endgames for the average-to-good player. Intermediate–advanced. Algebraic (originally issued in descriptive notation in 1974 and 1977).

37. ———, & Alexander Kotov. **The Art of the Middlegame.** Penguin Books, 1964; reprinted Dover, 1989. Fascinating essays by Keres on defense and analysis and by Kotov on attacking the King and central Pawn positions. Intermediate–advanced. Descriptive.

38. Kmoch, Hans. **Bled 1931 International Chess Tournament.** Translated from the original 1934 Russian edition by Jimmy Adams. Caissa Editions, 1987. Alekhine's greatest victory (by a margin of 5 1/2 points!) over a very strong field, fully and profoundly annotated by Kmoch, who was the arbiter (director) of the event. Advanced. Algebraic.

39. ———. **Pawn Power in Chess.** David McKay, 1959; reprinted Dover, 1990. A great, and enjoyable, middlegame classic. Intermediate. Descriptive.

40. Kotov, Alexander. **Grandmaster at Work.** American Chess Promotions, 1990. A great attacking player's best games, most instructively annotated. Arranged thematically rather than chronologically. Intermediate–advanced. Algebraic.

41. ———. **Think Like a Grandmaster.** B. T. Batsford Ltd., 1971. A modern middlegame classic, extremely useful in learning to calculate accurately and evaluate positions correctly. Intermediate–advanced. Descriptive.

42. König, Imre. **Chess from Morphy to Botvinnik.** G. Bell & Sons, 1951. Uses complete, illustrative games to describe the strategical evolution of four major openings—Ruy Lopez, King's Gambit, Queen's Gambit and English—over a hundred-year period. A truly wonderful book. Intermediate. Descriptive.

43. Krabbe, Tim. **Chess Curiosities.** George Allen & Unwin, 1985. A fantastic collection of oddball facts about strange chess positions, amazing games, peculiar chess records, etc. Intermediate–advanced. Algebraic.

44. Larsen, Bent. **Larsen's Selected Games of Chess 1948–69.** G. Bell & Sons Ltd., 1970. The best games of probably the most original modern player, quite entertainingly explained. Intermediate–advanced. Descriptive.

45. Levy, David. **Play Chess Combinations and Sacrifices.** Oxford University Press, 1980. One of the best combination books ever written. Intermediate. Algebraic.

46. Littlewood, John. **How to Play the Middlegame in Chess.** RHM Press, 1974. An excellent teaching manual, with very pertinent chapters on how each piece functions in the middlegame. Intermediate. Descriptive.

47. Mednis, Edmar. **How Karpov Wins.** David McKay Co., Inc., 1975; enlarged, corrected edition, Dover, 1994. A great instructional work, using the games of perhaps the most unremittingly logical of all the world champions. Intermediate–advanced. Descriptive.

48. ———. **Strategic Chess: Mastering the Closed Game.** Summit Publishing, 1993. A first-class book on correct middlegame planning, with 30 deeply analyzed games grouped by opening. Intermediate–advanced. Algebraic.

49. Minev, Nikolay. **French Defense: New and Forgotten Ideas.** Thinkers' Press, 1988. Instructively arranged, imaginatively annotated collection of 450 games with this important opening. Intermediate–advanced. Algebraic.

50. Nimzovitsch, Aron. **Chess Praxis: The Praxis of My System.** Printing Craft Ltd., 1936; reprinted Dover, 1962. A sequel to *My System* (below) and equally valuable! Intermediate–advanced. Descriptive.

51. ———. **My System.** Harcourt, Brace & Co., 1930; reprinted Hays Publishing Co., 1991. One of the all-time great classics on every aspect of the game. Intermediate–advanced. Algebraic.

52. Nunn, John. **Tactical Chess Endings.** B. T. Batsford, 1988 (2nd, corrected edition). An amazing collection of fantastic endgames from practical play, by the most respected contemporary theoretical chess writer in English. Advanced. Algebraic.

53. ———, & P. C. Griffiths. **Secrets of Grandmaster Play.** B. T. Batsford Ltd., 1988. Twenty-five of Nunn's most exciting games, chosen particularly for their didactic value, painstakingly analyzed by Nunn and explicated by Griffiths. Advanced. Algebraic.

54. Pachman, Luděk. **Decisive Games in Chess History.** Pitman Publishing, 1975; reprinted Dover, 1987. A fine compilation of many of the most important games in the modern history of chess (1870–1972), with very instructive notes. Intermediate–advanced. Descriptive.

55. Pandolfini, Bruce. **The ABCs of Chess.** Simon & Schuster, 1986. A delightful collection of 50 of Pandolfini's best articles on all-important aspects of chess instruction. Beginner–intermediate. Algebraic.

56. ———. **Pandolfini's Endgame Course.** Simon & Schuster, 1988. One of the best, and most accessible, introductory books ever written on essential endgame knowledge. Beginner–intermediate. Algebraic.

57. ———. **Weapons of Chess: An Omnibus of Chess Strategy.** Simon & Schuster, 1989. A terrific book for the player who knows how the pieces move, but not much else. Beginner. No notation, although the squares themselves are referred to algebraically.

58. Polugayevsky, Lev. **Grandmaster Preparation.** Pergamon Press, 1984. A great modern player's best games, engagingly and instructively annotated. Advanced. Algebraic.

59. ———. **The Sicilian Labyrinth.** 2 volumes. Pergamon Press, 1991. Superb delineation of the basic ideas behind the most popular modern defense to 1. e4. Intermediate–advanced. Algebraic.

60. Reinfeld, Fred. **The Human Side of Chess: The Great Chess Masters and Their Games.** Hanover House, 1960. A beautifully written, extremely interesting and very subjective history of the world champions from Anderssen to Euwe, by a man who understood more about the great players in chess history than many so-called historians. Beginner–advanced. Descriptive.

61. ———. **Reshevsky on Chess.** By Samuel Reshevsky [sic]. The Chess Review, 1948. A superb biographical games collection, now known to have been ghostwritten by Reinfeld! Intermediate–advanced. Descriptive.

62. ———, editor. **The Treasury of Chess Lore.** Arco, 1955. A treasure-trove of history, humor, anecdotes, etc. Beginner–advanced. Descriptive.

63. ———, & Reuben Fine. **Lasker's Greatest Chess Games 1889–1914** (formerly titled *Dr. Lasker's Chess Career*). Black Knight Press, 1935; reprinted Dover, 1963. Profound notes to the most profound player's games. Intermediate–advanced. Descriptive.

64. Renaud, George, & Victor Kahn. **The Art of the Checkmate.** Simon and Schuster, Inc., 1953; reprinted Dover, 1962. Collection of 299 examples of standard mates clearly defined and demonstrated. Intermediate. Descriptive.

65. Réti, Richard. **Masters of the Chessboard.** Whittlesey House, 1932; reprinted Dover, 1976. A timeless classic, interpreting the history of chess strategy through the styles of the best players from approximately 1850 to 1930. Intermediate. Descriptive.

66. ———, & H. Golombek. **Réti's Best Games of Chess.** G. Bell & Sons, 1954; reprinted Dover, 1974. A beautifully written "labor of love" about one of the greatest *artistic* grandmasters. Intermediate–advanced. Descriptive.

67. Romanovsky, Peter. **Chess Middlegame Combinations** and **Chess Middlegame Planning.** American Chess Promotions, 1990, 1991. Superb translations by Jimmy Adams of these classic Russian textbooks. Intermediate–advanced. Algebraic.

68. Shereshevsky, M.I. **Endgame Strategy.** Pergamon Press, 1985. A Russian coach's patient, carefully thought out approach to learning how to evaluate and play typical endings. Intermediate–advanced. Algebraic.

69. Silman, Jeremy. **How to Reassess Your Chess.** Expanded 3rd edition. Summit Publishing, 1993. Teaches how to recognize and understand the essential features of most important middlegame, and many endgame, positions. An exceptionally well conceived book, profusely illustrated with fine examples. Intermediate. Algebraic.

70. Soltis, Andrew. **Openings Ideas and Analysis for Advanced Players.** 2 volumes. Chess Digest, 1991 and 1992. A lucid discussion of the evolution of modern opening theory since World War II, with many fine, illustrative games. Really an excellent sequel to König's *Chess from Morphy to Botvinnik.* Intermediate–advanced. Algebraic.

71. ———. **Pawn Structure Chess.** David McKay Co., Inc., 1976. An excellent middlegame work—a perfect sequel to Kmoch's *Pawn Power in Chess.* Intermediate–advanced. Descriptive.

72. Speelman, Jon. **Best Chess Games 1970–1980.** George Allen & Unwin, 1982. Careful selections from this fertile period, with copious commentary. Advanced. Algebraic.

73. Tal, Mikhail. **The Life and Games of Mikhail Tal.** RHM Press, 1976. One of the greatest, and most instructive, autobiographical games collections ever written. Advanced. Descriptive.

74. ———. **Tal–Botvinnik Match for the World Chess Championship 1960.** RHM Press, 1980. A remorselessly honest and instructive appraisal of his upset victory by the most brilliant tactician of our era. Advanced. Descriptive.

75. Tarrasch, Siegbert. **The Game of Chess.** David McKay Co., 1935; reprinted Dover, 1987. Another famous classic, with magnificent sections on both the middlegame and endgame. Beginner–intermediate. Descriptive.

76. ———. **St. Petersburg 1914 International Chess Tournament.** Edited by Dale A. Brandreth. Caissa Editions, 1993. A seminal tournament book about this legendary event in which the aging Lasker was still able to defeat his future conqueror Capablanca. Written by a great player and teacher. Advanced. Algebraic.

77. Tartakower, S. G. **My Best Games of Chess 1905–1954.** 2 volumes. G. Bell & Sons, 1953, 1956; reprinted in one volume by Dover, 1985. A delightful and entertaining autobiographical games collection by one of the wittiest and most original grandmasters. Intermediate–advanced. Descriptive.

78. ———, and J. Du Mont. **500 Master Games of Chess.** G. Bell & Sons Ltd., 1952; reprinted Dover, 1975. A standard, classic collection of great chess from 1788 to 1938. Intermediate–advanced. Descriptive.

79. Timman, Jan. **The Art of Analysis.** RHM Press, 1980. A modern classic, showing how a top world-championship contender turned himself from a merely good annotator into a profound one. Advanced. Algebraic.

80. **U.S. Chess Federation's Official Rules of Chess.** Fourth edition (or subsequent editions). Edited by Bill Goichberg, Carol Jarecki and Ira Lee Riddle. David McKay, 1993. Essential for the rules of tournament play. Beginner–advanced. Algebraic.
81. Vukovic, V. **The Art of Attack.** Pergamon Press, 1965. By deeply analysing many classical attacking masterpieces, this classic treatise outlines the prerequisites for successful attacking play. Intermediate–advanced. Descriptive.
82. White, Alain C. **Sam Loyd and His Chess Problems.** Whitehead and Miller, 1913. A seminal work on the preeminent American problemist. With 744 problems. Advanced. Descriptive.
83. Whyld, Ken, & David Hooper. **The Oxford Companion to Chess.** Second edition. Oxford University Press, 1992. Despite a slight anti-American bias, this is still by far the best and most accurate encyclopedic work on chess history in English. Beginner–advanced. Algebraic.
84. Wilson, Fred. **A Picture History of Chess.** Dover Publications, Inc., 1981. An attempt to illustrate the history of chess through pictures of the most important players and events, with much informative commentary. Beginner–advanced. Descriptive.
85. Znosko-Borovsky, Eugène. **The Art of Chess Combination.** Chatto & Windus, 1936; reprinted Dover, 1959. A classic treatise on combinational ideas. Intermediate. Descriptive.

Index

DOVER BOOKS ON CHESS